Beatitudes

Also by Herménégilde Chiasson
in English translation

Lifedream: a play
(translated by Jo-Anne Elder)

Cape Enrage and *Alienor* in *Angels & Anger:*
Five Acadian Plays
(edited and translated by Glen Nichols)

Available Light
(translated by Wayne Grady)

Conversations
(translated by Jo-Anne Elder and Fred Cogswell)

Climates
(translated by Jo-Anne Elder and Fred Cogswell)

The Magic Rug of Grand Pré
(translated by Barbara LeBlanc and Sally Ross)

Beatitudes

Herménégilde Chiasson
Translated by Jo-Anne Elder

GOOSE LANE

Cover photo by Tina Lorien, istockphoto.com
Author photo by Marcia Babineau
Cover design by Julie Scriver
Book design by Kent Fackenthall with the collaboration of Herménégilde Chiasson
Printed in Canada
10 9 8 7 6 5 4 3 2

Library and Archives Canada Cataloguing in Publication

Chiasson, Herménégilde, 1946-
[Béatitudes. English]
   Beatitudes / Herménégilde Chiasson; translated by Jo-Anne Elder.

Poems.
Translation of: Béatitudes.
ISBN 978-0-86492-486-5

   I. Elder, Jo-Anne II. Title. III. Title: Béatitudes. English.

PS8555.H465B4313 2007   C841'.54   C2007-904308-9

Goose Lane Editions acknowledges the financial support of the Canada Council
for the Arts, the Government of Canada through the Book Publishing Industry
Development Program (BPIDP), and the New Brunswick Department of Wellness,
Culture and Sport for its publishing activities.

Goose Lane Editions
Suite 330, 500 Beaverbrook Court
Fredericton, New Brunswick
CANADA E3B 5X4
www.gooselane.com

Blessed are the meek, for they shall inherit the earth.

The Gospel According to St. Matthew

When we die, is it true that we can touch the blue of heaven?

Gabrielle Savoie, five years old

I pity humanity, I wish it were good, because I cannot separate myself from it; because it is myself; because the evil it does strikes me to the heart; because its shame makes me blush; because its crimes gnaw at my vitals, because I cannot understand paradise in heaven nor on earth for myself alone.

George Sand, letter to Gustave Flaubert
The George Sand-Gustave Flaubert Letters
translated by A. L. McKenzie, 1921

For Martha Babineau,
around a table to celebrate once more and forever the passage of
time, the wondrous gift of unassuming love through the changes of
the seasons, and the warmth that connects me to you through her,

Gérald Leblanc,
for our erratic paths, for the verbal intolerance of leaving anything
hanging during the time we fought together, discussions on the
state of the world, strategies for the here and now, and especially
for the words that we always carry around in our hearts and will
carry for a long time yet, I hope, from one creation to the next,

Pierre Bernier,
for his calm, his friendship as silent and sincere as the forest that
circles our lives, his capacity to perceive the ridiculous, and his
unfathomable impatience so close to the depths,

Jean-Marie Morin,
for the last night when the door opened to let you enter into the
light, while we could think of nothing to say except the silly words
that have stayed with me, the walk across the forest when we fell
as we carried you in our arms, the darkness out of which you
spoke to us, and the way of looking up towards heaven to see
us and hear us as far as the stars,

Gail Boyd,
for the winters of arranging places and worlds, voices and faces
filled with trust, and the way she left in each one the signs of her
grace, her compelling, generous and genuine goodness, and an
elegance that time could not wear down,

Guy Duguay,
for his irreverent, provocative, and wilful determination to leave
a sign, a mark, fragile traces to let everyone know, forever and
always, that we existed,

Beatitudes

those who raise their heads in astonishment at the
raucous cry of birds,

those who await the end of twilight,

those who ceaselessly leaf through catalogues and
order nothing from life,

those who sleep on their side, waiting for the pain
to subside in a single sip of water,

those who believe it is time to bear their misery,
smiling through the procession of painful stupidities and
offering atonement for the fullness of errors that are, in
truth, so forgivable,

those who weep and find no consolation, confusing
love with bitter anger in the loose thread of unravelling
clothes,

those who walk ahead even though the wind blinds
them,

they are, certainly, on their way to heaven;

those who lean heavily over countertops, whispering
about their jeopardized affairs,

those who find their keys in the bottom of plastic bags
they were about to throw out,

those who carry their food home in taxicabs,

those who stand up in public meetings where they
believe they have recognized their lives put on display in the
broad light of day,

those who pretend to be outraged by those who sing
out resignation in a borrowed tongue,

those who carry the discomfort of defeat in half-smiles
stained by underlying rage,

those who clown around in hard hats too heavy for
their bird-like heads,

those whose hands lift into the air as if separate from
their bodies, as if sketching into thin air thoughts they hope
will one day be written in indelible ink,

those who carry their children like slumbering
rivers, living poetry, acts of faith through the soundproof,
overheated corridors of modern buildings,

those who apologize profusely before slipping away
into the subdued obscurity of an unavoidable solitude from
which there is no escape,

they, too, will see heaven;

those who sob in public, immodestly displaying their poverty and their rebellion,

those who walk in anger, with methodical steps, under drab coats along cold, grey beaches,

those who hold onto the fervent hope that one day they will find the objects they thought lost and buried forever in mud-soaked marshes,

those who mutter under their breath, wondering whether they have said what should have been said and whether they have been understood as though, once again, they are using a grimy sponge to wipe clean the constant, dreary hum that covers their voices,

those who play,

those who laugh,

those who read,

they, too, yes, they are promised heaven;

those who consolidate their impenetrable positions, tottering on the rickety ladders of their ever-compromised power,

those who stop to contemplate the multi-coloured transformation of trees,

those who walk in the fog, lugging disappointments that feel heavier with every step they take, sorrows that weigh heavier by the minute,

those who dismiss the obscurity of all the sleepless nights of doubt, the accumulating sting of sad nights, and show a gaze washed neat in the after-effects of a deplorable blindness,

those who follow the latest trends in beauty, collapsing under the burden of their own unsightly appearance, attempting to craft something out of their tentative visions,

those who care for those who are sad, spineless, and ambitious, who live on credit and are bent over the indecent crutches of their dependence,

those who gather around vending machines, still under the cloud cover of sleep, debating the shameful prices of unpalatable drinks,

those who repair electrical circuits, who build bridges, who utter blasphemies in foreign languages, who know the feeling of hitting rock bottom, who understand impatience, who let themselves be seduced by the curves and caprices of fortune,

those who come to terms with authority figures,

those who reach the front and are unable to rally their strength under their washed-out, worn-out trench coats,

those who show patience, stretching out their hands under hot-air vents,

those who cross their arms with a pleading, unfocused timidity, those who sleep on beds too high off the ground, pushing away the memory of the chilly nights of childhood,

those who lower their eyes to watch as the anger they have spit out is absorbed into the ground,

those who close windows against the cool breeze of another autumn, rediscovering their past like an old piece of clothing in the vague, velvet perfume of a stray gust of air caught in a hotel bedroom,

those who speak to be heard and those who shout to be forgotten,

those who ask after you and smile indulgently at your plans, at your inventiveness, and who will come to appreciate the perpetual enigma you are about to become,

those who mechanically place chairs on tables and wipe clean the untiring tile of their insomnia with the waters of daily life,

those who find traces of their former loves in cardboard boxes, discovering a vague charm in their outdated nostalgia,

those who kneel for a moment in public places, ignoring the chairs they are offered,

those who eat quickly, who stop at traffic lights, who calculate their assets while forecasting their prospects,

those who do word searches to discover their destiny, who invest time in crossword puzzles, who look in them for the strength and grave power of magic words,

those who mince their words, who weigh their words, who look for the right ones,

those who close their eyes, who give themselves over to the sun, opening their arms to the consummate fire of its embrace,

those who put their life back at the starting gate,

those who hold their coat collar tight around their throats while their hands grow numb with cold,

those who transport heavy equipment, who forever dream of engraving their futile, frustrated acts on fragile plastic bands rolled into a spiral,

those who deposit their humble, unpretentious lives into nylon bags stretched beyond the limit, their hands marked by the weight of their goods,

those who raise flags like solidly anchored opinions, agendas, reports, positions, and social platforms, fighting against the ferocious wind that shakes them as they grip the rails of balconies,

those who work at night and sleep during the day,

those who dance for money in front of men who, during one more warm beer, cry out at the miracle when they imagine they've found the river that flows forever between a woman's legs,

those who slowly hang up the telephone as they learn of the long-distance collapse of the world close to them, the light and sounds dimmed by the emptiness filling in around them, taking up all the room, letting everything slip away in a colossal, ill-fated landslide that so abruptly takes over an entire life,

those who put their future recovery into jeopardy by swallowing massive doses of intoxicants,

those who carry their love at arm's length,

those who brim over with tenderness and their overwhelming illusions,

those who unclench their fists with the idea that, like swimmers, their open hands will speed up their pace as they navigate the currents of circulating air,

those who put out their hand and hope they'll get the exact change for the train,

those who lock the door and leave the keys inside,
distracted by something they can neither avoid nor explain,

those who stand up tall in the middle of the lawn,
heads shaved clean, a cigarette in hand, and wait patiently
for someone to stop and listen to the unending flow of
words that reconfirm and reaffirm their authoritative
confusion,

those who find themselves under lights that radiate
with splendour into the unbounded night,

those who cry for help into microphones, believing
they'll hear in their amplified distress the exalted legacy
of a swallowed-up past,

those who talk too fast, who craft makeshift images,
who remember the gaps of memory that need to be filled
again and again in writing, who scribble stories on bits of
cardboard forgotten along the way,

those who lie openly, compensating for their
anonymity with the role they claim to have played in alleged
adventures, which contributed to their apparent failure, or
so they say,

those who return from afar,

those who are not without knowledge,

those who are supposed to understand,

those who never let on,

those who slip in and out of the shadows,

those who bond with emptiness,

those who get lost in the details,

those who have seen because they believed,

those who are not prophets in any country,

those who gaze with the naked eye and see the strange,
blinding beauty of those who miraculously step out of the
shadows,

those who hear the still, small, intimate sounds of things, whose glory stems from spreading the word, who are coming to terms with reality, who are born under the right star, who walk lightly along the edge of emptiness, who radiate an awe-inspiring confidence,

those who hang onto the same notes, who hum them all day long, who push them out of their minds and let them back in unwittingly, unable to erase them,

those who declare their awkward confidences in the midst of an anonymous, sleepwalking crowd,

those who make faces, who tell jokes, who make fun of themselves on the off chance they might hear the crystalline sound of their children's laughter just one more time,

those who greet strangers, hoping to catch, in this simple random gesture, a sign of a common path,

those who come to meet you and candidly admit the poverty of their lives, the inadequacies of their hearts, the obligations of an everyday life exhausted by overcoming what cannot be overcome, a childhood by default, and their blind faith in begging for help from ordinary passersby,

those who smile at the naïveté of those who subject their reality to the absolute register of their dreams,

those who imagine themselves to be prosperous, important, and seductive, imposing, lofty, and irresistible,

those whose laughter catches others off guard and charms them with its generous honesty and its seductive liveliness,

those who pledge to never again bend down to pick up the penny destined to bring them luck,

those who turn away from the merchants of hope, pushers of good-humoured propaganda and other toxic products,

those who line up at the counters of poverty, whose
very existence demands a constant effort that exhausts body
and mind,

those who stare at the landscape, aimlessly sprinkling
salt on their tasteless sustenance,

those who fall asleep alone on the damp bed of
distress, shooting bullets into the hearts of those who
commit the error of getting too close to them,

those who inevitably curl into a fetal position when
they have to take a seat,

those who step down from their pedestals and find
themselves on the humble level of confessions as disarming
as they are disconcerting,

those who stare at the ground in search of essential
objects, forgetting the places of eternal deliverance as
they look for the keys among the blades of grass or grains
of sand, aware that it's late and they had better return to
the shelter from which they had earlier escaped, where it
seemed as if they had been awaited for all time,

those who sit and listen helplessly to the silence of
those who muffle their cries, who head slowly and hesitantly
towards cliffs from which they might fly like angels,
taking wing on gusts of wind that blow above the apparent
emptiness of their unsteady lives and uncertain loves,

those who live their lives with the grace of birds,
following in formations traced in advance through clouds
and seasons, leaving at the appointed time to fly across the
world at full tilt,

they, too, will take flight towards heaven, lifting the
burden of a bitterness that had planted them like stakes
into the ground of their own histories, so often heavy and
waterlogged,

they will meet the tenuous finality of destinies merging into a total release from all urgency,

they will rediscover the hidden face of a shimmering paradise standing with the shadows that inhabit the night, expending exhausting efforts to follow them, seeking comfort in obscurity, remembering the plan begun long ago, of which they have eventually become the executors, the heirs, and the beneficiaries;

those whose every breath is filled with good humour,
those who run into old friends,
those who worry about the way the wind is turning,
those who invent new ways to capture the superb
contrasts of an autumn sky, who let themselves be carried
away by the moon when it hastens under a diaphanous veil
and fades into that grey light, the worrisome consequence
of a destiny that sometimes envelops us when night falls,
those who were once princes and later banished from
their kingdoms for committing the odious crime of love,
those who can decode the key to constellations, fatally
deciphering the clues to the causes of timeless fears,
those who call for help from their cars, impatient
when their cellphone batteries wear out and the connection
is lost,
those who examine their reflection in an intense effort
to detect non-existent hints of aging,
those who watch their step as they walk, carefully
hiding their bruised hearts under an armour of leather,
those who tell lavish lies, believing that they will
release themselves from the obscure mystery of misery,
those who ask where they will turn when all the doors
have closed,
those who glimpse among the floating clouds the sure
signs of impending reconciliation,
those who wait patiently, dancing with their shadow
facing the walls, watching their lives unfold and vanish
in the smoke of cigarettes, imagining themselves in total
control of their destiny, commanding their heavy hearts to
make amends, knowing that time will heal their wounds,
casting aside happiness, pretending to leave and staying all
the same, standing transfixed in the chaotic wind of despair,
unable to stick the left-over shards back together, unable

to reproduce the magic of the moment when the cold lost its grip on them, when the sky reached out towards them, when life resurfaced beside them, when the world repaired itself before their eyes,

those who take off their coats and bare their bodies, marketing them like retro or resale goods,

those who roll up their sleeves,

those who catch their breath,

those who stare at a distant point in an otherwise empty space,

those who keep coming back from the same endless and disappointing journey,

those who close once again and forever the crates of sorrowful memories,

those who know and say nothing,

those who knew and did nothing,

those who settle their affairs and can no longer bear to shiver under the constant, icy blows that afflict them,

those who sing at the top of their lungs during storms,

those who read cookbooks and have no one to cook for,

those who sit near the door, always expecting the worst, those who choose to laugh at their bad luck instead of weeping with constant despair and foolish bitterness,

those who dim the bright intensity of lamps to bring the light down to the level of their humble, obscure lives,

those who light candles,

those who make love to keep warm,

those who are euphoric about the mystery of snow crystals, delicately carrying home their unique fragility on woollen mittens,

those who pause to notice the way the sun shatters against the clouds and shoots into the horizon a shower of rays which, some believe, utter calls to the universe,

those who fight with all their strength against hands
that want to hold them,

those who continue to trust in their blind desire that
their pain will dissolve in the burning water of overheated
baths,

those who want only to withdraw behind a screen of
beauty, believing that the blinding brilliance of its armoured
gold veil might finally vindicate them for the lives they once
had, when they thought they were resigned and willing
tenants in an obscure and tenacious misery,

those who forget their gloves and go out into the night
with bare hands, delivered, finding themselves under the
endless starlit canopy of the cold that will eventually reach
them,

those who resign themselves to being robbed in broad
daylight of the meagre earnings of their labour,

those who live under the weight of injustice,

those who lose their way and, yet, keep walking,
despite everything, sending their gaze through the night
towards that spark, that ray of light, keeping their eyes fixed
on it, and imagining that it will grow into an awe-inspiring,
all-consuming star,

they, too, hardened by their travels, have no choice
other than to keep on walking towards heaven, over the
ruts and pitfalls, their hearts becoming lighter and lighter,
larger and larger, with each step as they wander unnoticed
and without fear through one detour after another, choosing
paths at random, crossing through the thoughtless rumours
and mindless cruelties of the lower world;

those who call in the middle of the night to tell you about an unforgivable crime, an unavoidable weakness, their dependence, their confused desires, and their inability to walk away, sacrificing any scrap of dignity they have managed to save from the uncontrollable influence of alcohol, drugs, and desire,

those who listen to their own breath and carefully measure their heartbeat, marvelling at their flawless connection to all that lives and endures,

those who play along, who play deaf, who play dead, who play the clown, who play the game of life, who play fair or foul, who play the monster, who play tough,

those who nurture the hope of a clean break and who remain, waiting and hoping for a happy ending, a sign, a miracle or, better yet, a permanent release that only time can bring,

those who imagine themselves to be powerful, who are gripped by an underhanded ambition to furnish their solitary space, who ignore the signs offered by their lives in the swelled sweep of its trajectory and the scope of its mission,

those who never tire of gambling with their fortunes and placing their destinies in the shaky hands of fate,

those who travel around the world,

those who are in perpetual motion,

those who burst out in overstated glee,

those who are about to reach the finish line and abandon the race before they have had time to enjoy the promises of glory,

those who draw out their drinks as long as possible, who watch ice cubes floating and then melting nonchalantly in the bottom of yet another glass, those who shelter a troubled and unspeakable world deep within themselves, knowing all too well that they have forever compromised the happiness of those whose heart they once held in their hands and whose world they once held in their arms,

those who venture out in snowstorms, forgetting the fragile, permeable boundary that once stood between pain and danger, purity and silence, warmth and oblivion,

they, too, in the unpredictable and perpetual movement of waves, unique and vast like the movement of the sea, identical to the way time bends the curve of our expectations as we move from one place to another, elegant as the blind movement of clouds under the deep blue of the universe, crossing the sky from one side to the other and moving with open hands, closed hearts, and awestruck eyes towards the ultimate refuge of a paradise forgotten a thousand times over, an oblivion where all misery is swept into the spiral of time, the reference point where every imagining, however majestic or memorable, is reasserted in a sublime, timeless gesture of abandonment;

those whose faces, under the bruised mask of an ancient drama, are distorted by the dawning light,

those who awkwardly take off their hats to stammer their ill-defined requests,

those who have devoted their lives to the obscure fulfillment of a single obsession, stretching out to exhibit in the indignant night the heat stolen from the sun, the fruit of a long-sought and ongoing search undertaken on the untiring, tense, attentive body of love,

those who dance with their feet nailed to the floor, their hair flying out in all directions, shaken by a rage so deep it would send a tremor through every cell of their body if it were not for this convulsive gesture, this snapshot of planned revenge that protects them from the panorama of despair,

those who trade love for small change and splurge all day long in a constant urge to bail out humanity from its merciless debt load,

those who come from elsewhere and go somewhere else, knowing they have burned their bridges, disowned and discarded anyone who might have shown them how to clear a new path, repair an old one, or level out others for those who will come later, walking barefoot over the burning asphalt, defying pain and injustice,

those who run out of excuses,

those who refrain from making comments,

those who use discomfort as a pretext,

those who stand up and leave the table in disgust,

those who have nothing else to prove,

those who follow in wonder in the anonymous tracks left by predecessors unaware of the great beauty they have created, those who look for tiny objects gone missing with only the flickering light of matches that the wind takes pleasure in blowing out,

those who leave their plate on the window sill to give relief to those whose hunger never lets up,

those who stand too close to flames,

those who feel assaulted by daylight when it wraps itself around their profound nakedness,

those who listen with no hope of understanding,

those who forget to turn off the lights,

those who once again ask for directions,

those who walk in order to forget,

those who surprise themselves when they come across a desired presence in a makeshift stairwell, a nostalgic place where their entire childhood rises up to the surface, a space between sky and Earth where they developed the terrible habit of flying away,

those who laugh as they take off their hats, nonchalantly exposing their awkward charm and their daft grace,

those who close their eyes to picture their desire,

those who burst out in wild laughter to hide their shyness and mask their misfortune,

those who apologize for their unexpected absence, unable to refrain from spreading out their beauty in the very places they feel defeated,

those who speak in a whisper, aware of the need to stop the spread of dry, rough patches of prejudice,

those who stutter,

those who explain,

those who repeat,

those who listen,

those who hear,

those who daydream,

those who return,

those who reassure you by telling you that life is much better than anything that can be put into place to limit its course and who promise you their help, assuring you that money is only money,

those who know the secret place where happiness hides and who cover up their tracks when they visit,

those who scribble graffiti on their bodies with lead pencils, engraving their story in the secret depths of their skin, scratching themselves until they bleed, making a lie of pen and paper,

those who turn down the volume,

those who prick up their ears,

those who avoid looking askance at unhappiness,

those who go on and on about the hidden meaning of every word, who see the underside of the opaque decor, the underbelly of things, and who keep guard until justice is done,

those who wonder what should have been done so that the lessons of the past could be conveyed to the present,

those who invite strangers over with the explicit purpose of converting them to their own well-founded beliefs,

those who travel great distances only to arrive late in places where they are no longer expected,

those who eat with their hands,

those who drink straight out of the bottle,

those who have promised themselves that one day they will pay off their lives with a suitable revenge,

those who lie to soften misfortune,

those who erase years of bitterness and injustice with the disarming discretion of an unanticipated smile, they, surely, despite the frenetic race that pushes us along in the daily flow of absurdity that makes us worry in the nerve centre of paralyzing terror, will find a way to vanquish fear and, in exchange, will be given the magic words and the map of the torturous and tangled paths that will lead them to the gates of heaven;

those who use all their strength and all their patience
to open doors frozen shut by the frost,

those who wait, imagining dazzling excuses to avoid
sinking into bitterness,

those who painfully inch forward, seized by the
momentary distraction of a mechanical action, advancing
with care along the icy sidewalk,

those who lose concentration over the uncontrollable
and unpredictable noise of broken-down machinery,

those who grimace as they pull their hair into an elastic,

those who can no longer manage to rouse themselves,

those who stoke the fires,

those who recount, in minute detail, endless tales of
accidents from ancient dreams,

those who speak up, caught up in the dizzy stream
of secrets they are convinced others have shared only with
them,

those who position their hand in front of their face to
protect themselves from the sun,

those who become aware of their anonymity,

those who show, with laughter and stories to bolster
their confidence, insignificant photos of past moments of
happiness,

those who make new lives between fresh sheets,

those who have watched good fortune come so close
that, for an instant, they could bathe in its beneficent comfort,

those who tell sad stories that make others laugh until
they cry,

those who catalogue their souvenirs,

those who harbour a grudge against non-smokers,

those who drink and will always want one more for
the road,

those who sing naughty songs and can't imagine that
their giddy laughter will ever end,

those who get back to work, wondering if they'll
have enough time, if they are making a difference, if their
dedication will match their anticipation,

those who play cards,

those who repaint dingy walls,

those who add leaves to tables,

those who sit uncomfortably in their chairs,

those who organize themselves,

those who speak their minds,

those who wear themselves out,

those who collapse on countertops,

those who see the sun rise over the snow,

those who have relinquished the long-forgotten
carefree summers,

those who lower their eyes when you speak to them,

those who believe they are powerful, prominent, and
prosperous,

those who have built a world in miniature and are
getting ready to move into it,

those who have lost hope that the dreams they once
nurtured will one day come true,

those who recognize their reflection in the arabesques
drawn by frost on their windows, figures and landscapes
where they imagine themselves floating, leaving their world
to navigate the depths of their melancholy, like exiles adrift,

those who would have us believe that it's all for the
best, that things will get better, that everything is already
unfolding as it should,

those who drink coffee in their cars as they wait for the
windows to defrost,

those who walk with care on the impeccable polished floors of their overheated houses,

those who do up the hoods of their nylon, supposedly windproof, jackets,

they, too, are heading, with a slow and measured pace, towards heaven, whose breadth and depth they will never understand if not, perhaps, for an unconscious ancestral memory of a well-deserved eternal rest, the infinite purity of a road they devotedly keep clear even though it is plagued with pitfalls hidden under so much whiteness and richness and quietness, exaggerated and foreseeable, this common path, this irreversible movement forward;

those who sweep snow off the stairs,

those who pull off their gloves with their teeth,

those who catch their breath,

those who watch the snow fall,

those who warm their hands under their folded arms,

those who see their fuzzy portraits reflected in the
cold, shiny metal of warehouse doors,

those who read their newspaper, huddled up against
the door while their car warms up in the night,

those who look at their watches and wonder what
they've accomplished during all this time they've spent
waiting,

those who find their eyeglasses,

those who walk with care to avoid the spasms of pain
waiting to leap up and grab hold of them, to spread agony
viciously, all the way down their spines,

those who have trouble smiling, who can barely mask
the fact they have trouble accepting the idea,

those who look for misplaced objects with rage and
frantic despair, knowing they can't afford to replace them,

those who cannot keep their hands off surfaces that
seduce them and textures that intrigue them,

those who make promises they'll forget,

those who get ready to leave, pushed on by an
inescapable urgency, who come back to get something,
knowing full well they are late and that no one will forgive
them,

those who get distracted and abandon their food on
counters in public places,

those who read quickly and lose their train of thought
or the connection they should have made,

those who continue their speeches without a break,
without saying things everyone has the right to know,

those who put on their coats to forge ahead into the cold, satisfying a physical urge to propel cigarette smoke into the prohibited purity of winter's whiteness,

those who cross their legs, confident of the effect they are bound to produce on the men who watch them,

those who fantasize about the figures drawn on the ceilings by cigar smoke,

those who discreetly tie up their housecoats as they get ready to face the cold that has seeped into the cracks of their poorly insulated houses,

those who don't budge because they believe their stillness will help them get rid of the anger that tries their patience,

those who laugh emphatically and with bravado in public places to show that everything is going well, that things are definitely better, that they have now been released from the inconsolable grief that seemed to have locked them away forever,

they, too, will receive their misplaced paradise in exchange for all the moments of ecstasy, when they felt removed from the mean world they inhabited and from which they were dispossessed in a brutal moment of overwhelming sorrow;

those who blow on their hair to get it off their faces,

those who, without flinching, put on the clothes they used to wear when they were in love,

those who cuddle up out of habit to the warm body of desire and fall asleep in animal oblivion,

those who put on airs of mystery, who pose in incredible positions, who judge their bodies against the latest trends, who watch their scores rise, who let mystery hang in the balance, touching them with the tip of a silky transparent wing in a life lived without upheaval or remorse,

they, too, without asking any questions, without knowing why, and without really wanting to know, will see the gates of paradise open, the multitude of angels kneeling as they pass by, the power of salvation filling their bodies and radiating with glorious light, the magnificent bright light in the lofty expanse of heaven, in the firmament where alcohol no longer intoxicates the spirit, a new comet of ultramarine blue embroidered with silver, the intense blue of the night blending into the blue of day where the anguish of actions and supplications is magnified and tells us that, yes, salvation is within reach, it is at the gate, enter it and think about something else when there are prophecies of doom and laments for a multitude of scourges that will plague the land for, in truth, heaven is closer than we think, the universe reinvents itself in each instant, and stones lie mutely dreaming of the day they'll become birds;

those who, even at an early age, have built for themselves a paradise in the palm of their hand,

they, too, by a stroke of magic that turns dreams into happiness, having earned their heaven on Earth as well as their misery on roads slick with ice and snow, will know the joys of excess, will take up once more their earthly journey in the loftiest reaches of heaven, will become heavy as they cross the clouds of eternity to begin another paradise here below in the lowest of heavens and so on and so forth until the end of time, tireless workers labouring from dawn 'til dusk and from dusk 'til dawn, taking the others as witnesses and embracing them enthusiastically, walking alongside them with the exaggerated strides of solitude so that one day they might find themselves illuminated by reflections of rivers rushing to the sea, rivers where wounds are washed away, where sorrows are doused, and nightmares are erased forever;

those who wait for the advent of freedom's reign,

those who await the arrival of the impossible,

those who watch storms unfurl through the portholes of their overheated offices,

those who water their plants,

those who cut metal,

those who turn the meter back to zero,

those who calculate their contribution,

those who are banished from public places,

those who compile thick files, squandering their lives as they accumulate overwhelming evidence,

those who file their shattered and pathetic lives in grey metal filing cabinets,

those who need to engrave the chronicle of their exploits on the walls of washroom cubicles,

those who, wary of unforecast rain and early frost, brake at every turn and fret over the nerve-wracking and unforeseen condition of the road,

those who tear up traffic tickets and watch this confetti fall to the ground through the murky, fog-laden air of intractable anger,

those who, inadvertently or mistakenly, without checking their contents, toss out papers they will search for their entire lives,

those who change their diet,

those who sit in doctors' waiting rooms,

those who collect empty bottles in the ditches,

those who ask for a second opinion, who get informed, who read up on the subject, who are ready for the onslaught of questions, who recognize the music, who brag about their unflappable expertise, who make themselves sound solemn, deep, and, why not, perhaps even threatening in response to the insults that act as their security,

those who promise more than they can give,
those who let themselves get carried away,
those who play with fire,
those who long ago learned to navigate the troubled
waters of their shattered lives,
those whose intransigence has made everyone detest
them and who swallow their bitter sadness over a mistake
they can't figure out, atoning for something they didn't say,
choose, or do at the right time,
their lives will bring them back to their childhood
when they fall asleep, will enfold them and carry them
into the frost-flowered nights of glacial winters, will take
them to visit a heaven they have heard about so often and
for which they so deeply long to hold the key, so that they
can wander freely when life lays them back down in their
cold beds, abandons them in the morning in front of their
mirrors, their coffees, the highways that stretch out farther
and farther in front of them, trying in vain to show them
a detour over a new road where grace will smile on them
and where they can set down their ancient grudges and the
subjugated fear of hatreds that lurk ahead;

those who are indignant in the face of indifference,
those who wound themselves with sharp objects,
those who gobble their food,
those who make compromising statements,
those who imagine they are the victims of a conspiracy,
those who eat as they walk,
those who claim they are the safety deposit boxes of
truth,
those who fax their insults,
those who doubt,
those who insist,
those who sit at the steering wheel and cry,
those who write on blackboards,
those who fall asleep in the sun,
those who wait to be served in their own language,
those who have a radical change of attitude,
those who have seen your face somewhere before and
frantically search their memory for the sound of your name,
those who worry about the state of your health,
those who turn up the volume as loud as it can go to
prepare for the confusing and unpleasant noise that will
surround them,
those who can recognize in the grey sky the infallible
signs of an impending storm,
those who place their head against your forehead to
try to track the movements of your thoughts or to transfer
information or, simply, to try to get close to your soul,
those who stretch out their hands, imploring you to
help them up the steep slippery slopes they are preparing to
climb with or without you,
those who go and get wine,
those who do the shopping,
those who make supper,

those who move painfully, making their way slowly and cautiously over icy sidewalks,

those who turn around to make sure you haven't followed them with your eyes into their solitude,

those who can't get their keys to turn in the frozen locks of their houses,

those who touch up their lipstick,

those who carry their shoes in plastic bags,

those who never use a comb,

those who cut their own hair,

those who wipe the fog from their lenses,

those who write their names in the sand,

those who draw hearts and arrows or write risky confessions in the dust and dirt that builds up on car bodies,

those who use pointed objects to engrave graffiti into the cold frost that thickens on the windows of their houses,

those who insist on getting things out into the open,

those who share a deep respect for each other,

those who say yes with their eyes, offering the troubling and genuine confession of their vulnerable bodies,

those who leave flowers, love notes, flyers under the windshield wipers of cars in the parking lots of shopping malls,

those who hold your face in their hands as if to drink out of your mouth, as if from the source of an injury that cannot be repaired by any other means but in this intimate gesture, as distant as scripture and as moving as the sea,

those who care deeply about making sure the world is still and will always be a refuge of infinite warmth and constant comfort,

those who look up quotations in useless tomes of insipid and boring texts,

those who alter their voice when they recognize yours,

those who let themselves be distracted or seduced
by the trite, ordinary stories that others tell with excessive
detail and exaggeration,

those who find their words and whose world comes
into sharp focus during the predictable moment of
unbearable silence,

those who touch you in the deepest and brightest
moments of your life, whose white hands cut through the
protective and supposedly so impenetrable screen of your
indifference,

those who break their pact with food so that even their
flesh will bear the marks of their spurned love,

those who blame the whole human race, condemning
their own gender for submitting to men's desires, and who,
in the end, find themselves desiring a free-spirited life that
will be the serene proof they have fully accepted their own
solitude,

those whose eyes embrace everything around them,
wondering if in the emptiness, in the greenery, in the
silence, in the clouds inflated with heaviness, and in the
wind bearing the heavy breath that pushes them across
the sky, there might be a response, a way of crossing time
without being scraped and scarred, without losing for even
a moment the fluid and persistent grace that inhabits them,
this moment of escape, this patch of sky removed from
life, adrift on a forlorn river, an ice-floe in the middle of
summer, knowing full well that the sky is elsewhere, over
there, up there, behind the unfathomable and unbearable
white of the clouds that roll up and blanket the music they
believed they could hear and whose implacable distance
they measured, this hand that reaches out, trembling, trying
to contain an inexhaustible desire to be in heaven, the
natural home of happiness and love, where all betrayals are

now buried and absorbed into the deepest nether regions of the Earth, where they would have found their final refuge,

those who walk into the sea, searching the ocean floor to grasp its terrible depth, its salt-seasoned tears, its gaze saturated with wondrous riches, fixed on the very source of life, staring at it for hours at a time, trying any way possible to uncover the avowed fascination that has held it there for so long, the blue space, submerged, opaque under its origins, long before heaven appeared to us as an acceptable solution, occluded and distant, in the ages when we crawled on the sand, naked of any expectation, moving, moving simply forward, towards the trees, the vital green, towards the infinite blue, the low and cavernous music of our presence on Earth, on the shore of this sea that returns to us, tossing, showing us the beating heartbeat of the universe, this silence that covers everything in a perfect enigma, this walk over the waters, this return to the stars with their thunderous rhythms since their timeless departure, and, despite this heaven that keeps on stretching further, unfolding, exasperating us, and frustrating our desperate attempts to wear out the concept, to contain it, to imagine it as a rest area, like the sea of our origin, like a moment of distress, unmoving and calm, which would encompass both our journey back to our nebulous starting point and our everlasting home,

those who get up in the night and calculate the impact and importance of each gesture so as not to disturb the peace and quiet and especially the sleep of those who soundlessly wander along avenues lined with dreams,

those who light fires, ignited with illusions of the unbearably hot and lusty beginnings of adventures about which they believe they still have a foggy notion, those who burst out in astonished laughter as they make funny faces in a mirror that will hold the only record of their glee,

those who close the windows against the rain exploding in the tough, dense air of a summer as languid as it has been reassuring,

those who call out to you in public places, offering ridiculous merchandise produced under the cover of anonymity,

those who share with you, under the influence of an understandable fatigue, their anger, indignation, and weariness at the idea of doing the same thing again and again, repeating the same warnings, prophesizing the same ill fortunes, their image compromised by years of bitter battles and countless grey days, as if time, in its irresponsible and inconsequential course, could offer a form of justification to make the sacrifices worthwhile,

those who fold sheets,

those who make light work of chores,

those who chop vegetables,

those who let the water cool down,

those who ignore suggestions,

those who iron their clothes,

those who adjust their dishevelled hair in tinted windows, in the polished metal hoods of their cars,

those who do everything with obsessive accuracy,

those who smile to lighten the seriousness men instigate and spread like propaganda,

those who are disciples of no one,

those who come back from a long journey,

those who care nothing about the shortcomings of existence,

those who invent scandalous parallel lives to divert the attention of those whose expression has been invaded by gravity, whose hands constantly lay blame on hearts that are too generous, and who lavish love on lives which, some say, deserve the full blame for slipping into unconsciousness,

those who talk about their childhood, inventing legends in which they played the hero, battles from which they emerged unscathed, the unrelenting fear in the voices of their fathers who threatened them from high atop their foibles,

those who have gone down the same road over and over again, made the same mistakes and told the same lies, imagining themselves happy, imagining themselves strict, imagining themselves lost, and who can't help but go over the same memories, take the same path, repeat the same words, re-enact the same impossible, unruly, unsubdued gestures, and who long for nothing more than to see the world go back onto its axis and turn in the liberating splendour of migrating birds taking wing in formation, shooting across the heavens like arrows to lodge in the heart of all mystery and to rest where life takes back its meaning and the heart its irresistible and irreversible ascension,

those who slam on the brakes, gripped by the deafening urgency of something forgotten, suddenly take stock of the irreparable impact as they throw themselves into an abyss of makeshift solutions and backtrack to undo their travels,

those who negotiate with the forces of order to impose restorative solutions, unaware of the impact of their ploys,

those who worry about their descendants, knowing full well that life possesses an array of magic tricks, hides its cards, refrains from stepping in until the moment everything bursts apart in broad daylight, until unhappiness is made flesh, the distribution of trials, crosses, children's laughter camouflaging its lengthy manoeuvres,

those who carry the wounds and scars of disastrous accidents, their bones crushed by metal, who do their best to get over the pain of the monster that came to their rescue, opening its jaws to extract their living bodies while any hope was blotted out in the darkness that took its place all around them,

those who sketch the broad lines of their plans and can already picture themselves erecting cathedrals, drawing fabulous models out of nothing with a sweep of the hand, bringing to life images both grandiose and as vulnerable as rain,

those who come through great pain and trust blindly in the power of time to heal the injustice which has made them victims and hostages,

those whose tears prove that life has passed them by, that unhappiness keeps them under its thumb, and who have found shelter under the cover of their own pain, never pausing between outbursts of laughter or tears, taking upon themselves the difficult and risky burden of managing their own futile joys and infinite miseries,

those who read out loud, their voices seduced by words that come to them like unexpected lifeboats, words that transform themselves into precious gems embedded in the glossy white pages they venerate with effusiveness and the naive sincerity of children awed by the magic power of words that take them to the other side of the looking glass,

those who are discreet, always worried about making a gaffe, wondering if everything is proper, neat, and fitting, if everything is laid out in the splendour that others have come to expect, if everything is as it should be, those who imagine happiness in the form of a project, a dimension, a gift, a state of the soul, a moment of sublime reconciliation, a cosmic fusion, a heavenly body, an eruption, a collapse, a universe,

those who open doors for you, making allowances for the fact that you've forgotten your keys, for this weight you carry on your shoulders, this ball and chain pulling at your clothing,

those who bow ironically, who shower you with pompous clichés or call you sir or madam, unable to find any other way to express the curious respect that inhabits them and with which they have had to manufacture a suit of armour safe from you,

those who listen attentively to the songs of birds and can detect the melancholy tone of a drama from which humans have abstained,

those who recount with humour their past binges, their various struggles, and the countless plans that life uses to lead them astray,

those who are amazed by the ignorance and the stubbornness of an entire population lost in the secular lament of its exclusion, incapable of painting itself in anything but the washed-out pastels of regret that afflict you, you who have known so long, and cause you to heap insults upon those who should know, who are complacent, who defend themselves,

those who build vast systems of scaffolds to justify once and for all the need for dreams and ideas in the face of work's brutal devotion to deny the most fundamental rights of conscience, memory, and beauty,

those who have seen the images of another time and who have come away from them livid and haggard at the thought of such generosity being dismantled and betrayed, now absent from any speech, from any setting, from any mouth, of all the light that no longer knows how to shine, of all the ideas forgotten under the pretext of vague words whose meaning continues to escape us,

those who marvel at the forces of resistance constantly at work and who wonder about the origins of the ongoing efforts to stand up to giants so heavy and so weighty, trampling on the feet of the basic rights of those who are unaware of the fact that one day they will be defeated by a concert of discreet and tenacious rumours buzzing in the background that irritate and annoy them into arrogance as they busily measure the scope of their power, plucking out blades of grass along the way, pretending to ignore the voice that utters the same psalms and verses, a needle in the ear, caught in their throats and making their eyes run, that will one day find the crack that causes the collapse of the entire mausoleum erected to the sordid glory of tyrants, ogres, the thirsty beasts who once pledged with determination and devotion to devour them alive,

those who disdain what they haven't written themselves, ideas that didn't occur to them, words they didn't always say, and who, under the blows of unexpected drama, under the cover of their laughter and their beauty, plead guilty for this world that evades their grasp, for the strength that inhabits them and of which they believe themselves to be dispossessed, incapable of taking hold of their own lives and savouring the marvels they continue to bring into the world,

those who leave long messages, potentially as long as the reach of their pain, spreading out a profusion of words through the drone of the machine, when they end up coming to a hurried close, cutting to the chase, with abrupt declarations of love,

those who tie up their hair and think about how much
work is left to be done, uncovering faces that resemble
masterpieces of an ancient era, the delicate, silky ochre
light cast by madonnas and nymphs of the past, but who,
impervious to the desire they elicit, look at you with the
chaste eyes of another century, your century, to tell you that
there are pressing things to be done, that it is time to make
your move, that the world is not standing still, that you had
better take note right away of a certain number of details
because the day is fading and night is coming, a night where
we will have abundant time to lose ourselves in a world of
masterpieces from which they have fled,

those who turn away, unnerved by something they
have heard, by senseless male plans, by the random traps
laid out on the beaten path of daily life, by disproportionate
hopes, and by an ocean of misunderstanding that seems
to have swallowed them, as they walk the assigned road of
a life more inspiring and secure, though in a different way
than expected, and, in the end, more fulfilling,

those whose grace smiles through as they stand and
hold the door wide open for those who follow them, who
never notice the lengthy procession following the wait, their
wait, the wait of all of those whose wait is over and who
admit to themselves, sometimes aloud, that men have
become the caricature of a plan grander and more
important than they can fully remember, and which, in the
fragile, serene ecstasy of the door closing quietly behind
them as though pushed shut by a breeze, there is still and
always will be a need to find themselves in a form of a
march, to gather together to advance beyond hopes and
beliefs, a disorganized charity, the existence of a love, an
idea as old as the world, and the kindness of all those who,
beyond their expectations, in an obsession which incites

them to take action on things that they haven't completely
considered, whose scope and importance they haven't
properly measured, in spite of themselves, have finally
earned the heaven of their childhoods, the garden so
distant and serene that grownups used to talk about when
they asked embarrassing questions that went unanswered,
that they remembered their whole life long with inevitable
nostalgia, questions that now hardly make any sense and
make even less of a difference, except for the fact they have
followed the approximate path of a naive hope that has
grown patiently and deliberately day by day until it reached
the dimensions of paradise,

those who, as little girls, wanted to hear the voice and touch the hands of those who, as adults, grew faces right in the tree bark itself and unfolded skies of a strange grey colour above the charred forests of their memory,

those who place their hands on their hips so that photos taken in this pose would reveal the maturity of age and the resignation of days gone by,

those who fall asleep again after being victims of atrocious dreams where blood flowed in torrents,

those who fear strange insects that lurk in the grass and, from high above, lash out at the vulnerable zones of their absent-mindedly disrobed skin,

those who complain about the unrelenting vulgarity of men who keep repeating the same hilarious, childish gestures to show off a heavy depravity, at once laughable and regrettable,

those who change jewellery, clothes, and hairstyles, always worrying about whether their armour is resistant enough to shield them from new, formidable assaults in unknown situations,

those who show you, with feigned indecency, the marks left by the sun on the grain of their skin,

those who sit outside, withdrawing from the group in search of fresh evening air, night breezes, and the intriguing enigma of darkness,

those who worry that the world may not be in its place, that they haven't done enough to satisfy the men whose powerful gaze stirs their desire to play the perverse, demanding, intense, nerve-wracking game,

those who cry because they have been given the cold shoulder, when all they wanted was a hand to hold, the time to repair their confidence on a difficult, snow-covered road where they felt abandoned by everyone and mercilessly delivered to the indifference of those whose path swerved through the fog of consummate and inconsolable solitude,

those who wait insistently for the veil to lift on time, on unforeseen departures and promised returns, who are long resigned to the improbable idea of a future reconciliation when life will be ready to hand them the noisy, warm, modest home where they once lived,

those who keep busy shining light around them, aware that any stumble will be harmful and that darkness has done its time,

those who caress and admire costly items they will never be able to afford,

those who ask for medicine and will have to be satisfied with outdated prescriptions,

those who have lost their sense of smell and ask you to check whether the food they are about to prepare is about to go bad,

those who forget their clothes and are satisfied with the ones they have to borrow, creating a makeshift elegance, their hands poking out of sleeves like monstrous outgrowths, offering profuse gratitude for so much generosity, compensating for a slip of memory for which they can't forgive themselves when they find themselves with those who don't even notice,

those who assess their time, wondering if they'll have enough to go see the rocks that plunge like the pious into frigid waters or whether instead they shouldn't get completely lost on the ocean, taking their place at the prow of a boat and soaking up the scent of the sea and the blue of the sky, the sea breezes propelling them beyond emergencies so down-to-Earth, imagining themselves lifted high on its liquid surface and transported to the clouds at the speed of dreams, propelled by the wind to the gates of

paradise where they will enter cheerfully and go ashore in
the throne room where the God of their mistrust never
stops bursting into merciful laughter at the idea that
humans have given him such a grand role in the salvation
story, even though he often forgets his lines and is
constantly forced to ask them what he should do next, and
who, caught off guard by the arrival of these dishevelled
visitors, finds nothing to suggest other than to return to the
starting post, a little like someone who is merciful when you
are guilty beyond a shadow of a doubt, and who, ordering
angels to push your boat back over the sea of clouds from
which you had come, adjusting his all-powerful bathrobe,
confides to you that heaven is more complex than what
was shown in the faded pictures that they used to give you
and would lead you to believe that paradise could exist in a
sublime and deconstructed reading, forcing you to go back,
disappointed that you hadn't received the tablets of the
Laws, the new and improved version, as a disgraceful
consolation prize in this shoddy excuse for a paradise,

    those who check their bank books and wonder where
the money goes, who perform miracles under the cover of
anonymity,

    those who feed animals and make sure each one
receives a fair portion,

    those who explain to you, without flinching and in
excessive detail, why and how they were suddenly required
to agree to changes before being compelled to undertake
such unwieldy plans,

    those who with patience and resignation make
household appliances work, trying their best to hide their
servile vocation,

    those who meticulously hold onto the childish register
of their vacations, describing with fanciful freshness

the most commonplace and ordinary moments of their youthful existence for the benefit of adults blinded by the urgency of outrageously limited lives,

those who smile, hesitating between severity and surrender, at statements that leave them disarmed and perplexed, the voice of charm having won out over unpalatable and unreasonable arguments,

those who talk about animals with admiration, ascribing to them qualities forgotten by humans, excusing their obsessive vulgarity, inventing for them a life where courage has made room for play and wonder,

those who read in bed, aware of the fact that words will escape from them under the weight of sleep and that they will have the pleasure of letting themselves drift away towards universes where life and dreams merge under the cloudy, ill-fated invasion of exhaustion,

those who stop short in the middle of the conversation, negotiating a brief truce to discern the discomfort to which they have suddenly fallen victim,

those who make superhuman efforts to overcome the perpetual fear of their inevitable end,

those who use every means to keep their footing in the surging current of an insistent desire that keeps flooding, drenching, and pulling along their tired bodies,

those who shorten their life expectancy with futile exercises in the vague and constantly renewed hope of ridding themselves of the anguish that seeps out of their pores, leaking from under its dam of skin stretched beyond decent limits,

those who carry weighty and cumbersome objects, taking infinite care to sidestep obstacles, cracks, and the impeccable walls observing them in the silent tranquillity of their impenetrable solitude,

those who thank you profusely for ordinary gifts
without having an idea of their real cost,
    those who water plants,
    those who clean out the dirt stuck under their
fingernails,
    those who marvel at nature's mystery, at an
unassuming sprout that can give birth to an entire forest,
    those who tell stories in the colourless language
of conquests that once kept them alive, thanks to the
unrelenting charm of their beauty, when they walked down
dusty, deserted roads, imagining themselves in control of
their own deceptions, repeating the same promises, their
bodies compromised in an obsessive appeal, insisting on
making a gift of their beauty, putting it on public display
for all to see, so that both ends of their anonymous, dizzying
path could meet and so that they could find themselves in
other arms to sign other agreements, sealed with destiny's
kiss in the forest circling the house along this immeasurably
empty road, promising them the world for a song, love in
return for a few words, and heaven for the price of these
eyes which will clear away whole forests,
    those who turn around to smile at you, to show you
the traces of angels in the firmament, a safe passage to
heaven, opening wide the doors to let you inhale the sticky
smells and the oppressive heat shut up inside cars, leaning
against the burning metal, and letting in the sensations
of an encroaching hell warded off by a smile offered to
you and who, without knowing what to wait for, suddenly
remember nights in the backseats of taxicabs in the cities
they criss-crossed with you, who wonder if the evening air
is the same as the morning air, and who get used to the idea
that hell might also be like heaven, a never-ending absence
that digs in deeper and deeper like the steady hum of a

motor, a sensation that pulls away, moving the body along with it, branded with the mark of desire and with your voice drifting into the labyrinth of music, into the echoes of memories, into the colour of souls exhibited like a fragile, irresponsible monument to your absence, the remaining time inscribed in blurred letters in the register of pain and miracles, hell fading into the distance, heaven within the reach of lips and yet so far away from the hand that has not yet risked writing down the word, making the nebulous link between these worlds so that life will not lose itself nor be transformed into inevitable disorder,

those who sleep spread out in the middle of their dreams like others in a flower bed, picking up the dropped threads of their thoughts, poring over complicated books, reading and rereading the same passages, and, finally, giving up in disappointment, dropping the book from the hand marooned on the sheets, an enigma in the centre of a monstrance illuminating the room from one side of dreams to the other, a mirror where hope is given its due, where words are conquered, the heart going to great lengths to follow a life of simplicity, understanding, surrender, and, whenever possible, happiness, if only it weren't for this taste of heaven, and for only this to live for, without ever worrying even a little bit about dying, those who put on their glasses and contentedly watch the world take shape again, impeccably meaningful and immensely seductive, like the sun on the sea when it plays with water that was once so blue, covering it with a thin golden film on which all believe they might find their lost halo,

those who burst out laughing in public places, ignoring men casting irritated sidelong glances, judging them harshly for contravening some obscure convention, outraged by their lack of modesty, unaware of how ridiculous they are, falling victim to the laughter that makes them wobble on their pedestals,

those who sort through papers, who tally up figures, who find it scandalous that the cost of surviving keeps increasing,

those who walk ahead, out of breath, carrying at arm's length the fantasies of ordinary people, the meals that don't come, oblivious to the elegance that follows in their footsteps, the grimaces that cluster behind them like ribbons flittering in the violent winds in the wake of their nervous breath,

those who look around them for a sign of encouragement as emotion passes through them, who wonder if their trials are a collective plight or, rather, a sudden epiphany like those that afflict them in their heart of hearts, and who are, by definition, beyond the common reach of other mortals, sending us back to suspicious and troubling visions, a universe purely and properly imaginary, as secretive as a malicious confession, the world going back over its tracks and words returning to their inner source,

those who explain so awkwardly, so angrily, and with the confusion of victims, the faraway problems

that come from places they can no longer enter, mastering
with their shy grace an anger engendered at the price
of an incompetence as absurd as it is anonymous, this
unforgettable absence and inconsequential emptiness,
this unfair memory depriving them of memories,

      those who apologize for taking the time they take,
for taking up so much space, and who do all they can to
become small enough to remain unnoticed in the midst
of those who only have eyes for such deceptive innocence
and earthy elegance, skin offering itself up like a sudden
revelation under chests that swell up at the sight of men
whose leisurely eyes leer over suffocating furnishings, this
field of vision that must be crossed at all costs to draw back
fleeting attention and wait for the flow of the conversation
to subside, wait for the right time to set out on the path
towards the door out to fresh air, into the vertiginous
voyage of a vehicle void of meaning, the sun collapsing with
exhaustion against the windshield, sunglasses like armour
blocking out the peripheral bursts of daylight just before
solitude lowers itself, solitude at last, abundant solitude,
solitude as heavy as the stifling summer, solitude as mild as
the warm night stretching out as far as the horizon along
the highway, in the feverish music of the motor and beyond,
this possible and even probable exile that can't be located,
named, or fixed, except that it becomes farther, faster, more
blurred, and more forgotten as life's memories are forever
obliterated in the shock of the resounding noise,

      those who look around, casting a distracted,
momentary gaze, searching the walls for a mooring,
hunting down a notorious imperfection, a detail they may
have missed, waiting for machines to get used to the idea
of doing what they are meant to do, and who wake up
in a confused, compelling, convulsive spasm that warns

of a miracle newly accomplished, of the fact that Earth
is inhabited, or something as nebulous, as urgent, as
provocative, as an unexpected sigh, a heavy breath exhaled,
a jolt, a nervous shock, that pushes you to run as fast as
you can to witness the birth of an invoice or something
else just as monumentally trivial, something as eminently
unmemorable, because the land of mystery is still several
leagues away, stuck in the gears somewhere, and we don't
know how to find it, just as we really don't know the route
our dreams will take, ignoring the time and the weather,
we have engendered imperious machines, and soon our
own eyes will be a burden for us and faith will be rarefied in
our hurried progress, as we lose track of the path of angels
traced within us, which we persist in seeking on outdated
maps and along avenues that no longer exist,

       those who don't believe in salvation, who erect prisons
at the price of an exemplary patience rolled up in a cocoon
of sundry white threads glued together with a spew of
insults, and who curse themselves for the darkness they
think they have poured on the world, transcribed repeatedly
on kilometres of paper in ink soaked in mystery, who see
heaven far away, way out there, a tiny glimmer that will
soon be swallowed up by the night, and who have signed a
lifetime contract with an option for heaven, sent four copies
by registered mail for delivery within twenty-four hours,

       those who suffer through conversations without seeing
the point, who smile stiffly when they are spoken to so they
won't be left out, who reply half-heartedly and to the best of
their knowledge, and who have chosen to live with serenity
in the world in which they live, a world in the image of
heaven, of which they never doubt the existence even if
they have earned it a thousand times, without ever being
aware of it, by resting gently on life, their eyes full of mercy,

compassion, confidence, and serenity, by their propensity to embrace the world with their mystical, longing eyes, by the silence that confers upon them the ecstasy of a listening mind, the peaceful euphoria of surrender, and the bliss of finally returning to Earth once again,

those who cry softly in the morning air and wonder
what needs to be done to keep up with the struggle begun
the night before, the night before that, and their whole
life long, another day to fill, and who get up anyway, put
on their armour again, redo their makeup, and go back
into the panic zone, face to face with nature, which seems
to hold them accountable to humanity for the global
impoverishment of conscience,

those who become impatient with the slow progress
of absurd procedures, mindless statements, and the
maniacal will of men to control everything with a rigid set
of regulations and guidelines that have existed since the
beginning of time, that are set out in stone as hard as their
heads, penetrated only by ignorance and neglect,

those who carefully compile complicated and
condescending files, occasionally panicking over the idea
that life might make everything erupt and throw everything
up in the air as it strikes with the heavy blows of drudgery
and endless arguments about matters of consummate
insignificance, uttered, repeated, and noted ad nauseam,

those who go to bed early because they can no longer
bear to go over the same inventory of memories, to go
through the same motions, and to laugh at the same spots,

those who do without food to have the body they
always dreamed of, that they once thought they had, or that
once disappeared,

those who plunge into the still waters of idle oceans,

those who repeat the seduction ritual, only to surrender
to the arms of the wind,

those who painstakingly wrap gifts,

those who watch currents of air flicker through candle
flames on a windy summer night,

those who eat what others have left behind, insisting they are full and can't help but give in to the temptation of such superb flavours that irresistibly draw them into this prolonged manoeuvre swollen with excuses,

those who marvel at their dance steps, astonished at the ease with which the paths of their feet intersect,

those who steadfastly praise their love,

those who robustly laugh through torrential rainfalls,

those who let in animals and are tolerant of their fidgety and fussy charms,

those who worry about the late arrival of their guests,

those who lend their clothes and end up chilled and shivering in the freezing night, pretending that they can't stand the heat anyway,

those who get up in the middle of the night to answer the phone, laughing in their sleep, not knowing if they are on Earth or in heaven at this moment, and who can't get back to sleep and can only utter banalities, having given up trying to make sense, knowing that everything will be held against them for saying too much in this delirium punctuated by blanks and endless pauses,

those who persevere in their efforts at unskilled imitations of people no one can recognize,

those who lose their train of thought when they tell funny stories that no one finds funny,

those who get confused when they try to explain simple phenomena everyone else understands,

those who offer shelter to exhausted travellers,

those who get back on the road in the middle of the night,

those who listen to implausible stories,

those who get excited when they talk and stand up so their voice will carry and make up with their posture what they lack in sound and power, which they refuse to admit, in ideas, and probably in the firm desire to finally vanquish the damage caused by painful doubts,

those who have invested an unflappable confidence in the heavy, cumbersome books on their laps, crushing their knees while holding out the promise of opening their souls to the lightness of being,

those who trace directions on scraps of paper, marking in detail the route to take, the pitfalls to avoid, and the wonders to behold along the way,

those who wait in the rain for the latecomers they doubt will ever show up,

those who take photos, hoping to save in these images the feckless and fragile souvenirs of moments when they wanted only to become one with the surrounding crowd and prolong those euphoric moments far beyond their haunting temporal limits,

those who exchange addresses, remembering the unhappy times when they shared the same humiliation, laughing and singing in the face of the same misery, and determined to wipe from their memory years of bitterness towards those who forced them to slave away against their will,

those who bring books, signatures, and documents to prove they have indeed travelled back and forth to the heart of nostalgia and have returned safe and sound, their heads full of descriptions of worlds ravaged by time and of those they once knew and even loved,

those who greet you with signs of respect,
those who converse in a foreign language,
those who stand behind counters and serve,
those who do the dishes,

those who show visitors the secret place where they
hide their house key,

those who enthusiastically tell of ordinary activities
they were drafted to carry out,

those who take stock of their sudden wealth and their
long-held dreams, once hopeless and now possible,

those who watch, with resignation, as the tranquil
smoke rises from their morning cigarette,

those who offer the fruit of their labour with no hope
other than to contribute to the blossoming of a common
effort, to the work whose grandeur escapes them except
in a shared desire to see its fulfillment, its growth into
something they can't name, can't locate, can't schedule, but
which they can visualize, complete with its stumbling block,
its brilliance, and its satisfaction,

those who walk slowly, inhabited by a life about to
blossom, and who replenish the spaces they cross with a
sense of well-being and confidence in the idea that life is
still possible, that it is still viable, that one can make a gift
so immense to a world so threatening, so deceptive, and
sometimes so sublime, with splendours that people so enjoy
complaining about, and lamenting its cruelty, a world that
returns to haunt us in this blossoming under a woman's
skin, this life that clusters somewhere in the depths of their
bellies, this enigma that as children they cradled like a
primitive promise and that shows itself occasionally in the
broad light of day as though it were a mystery, as though
everyone had taken pains to hide it and to understand its
troubling, awkward presence and its moving, powerful
obsession, that stirs the entire human race, for which
there are no other solutions, no other dimensions, no
other compromises, and no other hopes, other than to
simply go back to the drawing board, to the time before

the memorable big bang that engendered all doubt, to the fragile galaxy multiplying outside of its nucleus, clinging to the surrounding membranes, irrigated with the blood of those who eternally move forward with an undeniable elegance, holding in their arms this weighty life that takes their breath away as they make their way down the road to paradise,

those who collapse on the ground, sinking their
cheerfulness into the hard surface of floorboards,

those who weep with despair, leaning on their arms
crossed into a mask over eyes in which there are no tears,

those who explode in an anger that throws a wrench
into the machinery of exploitation,

those who organize gatherings where they perform on
grandstands and theatrically denounce the aggressive tactics
of those who try their patience past its full and final limit,

those who walk, laughing, staggering, and laughing
even harder as they manage to get through the evening
in the company of caring friends who will find them a
makeshift bed with a cozy pillow to comfort them,

those who lean compassionately over the bodies of
others to slow down their movement and to avoid colliding
with those they might need to bypass in the overpopulated
bottlenecks of rush-hour traffic,

those who prove to be intransigent as they rigidly and
precisely apply the letter of the law,

those who smoke near doors they open nonchalantly,
blowing their smoke and ashes outdoors,

those who enjoy a woman's laughter and put on a show
so they can hear it again and again, its crystalline notes
tickling their night ears like evening breezes that make them
tremble with well-being and euphoria,

those who call in the middle of the night to tell you
about their moving discovery of an amazing and brilliant
talent, the joy of having witnessed a moment in which grace
and bliss merged, and when they may have glimpsed heaven
for a brief instant through the crack cut out of the night,
a wondrous space where it felt so good to stop so that the
moment could last forever for a while, the eternity of an
instant compounded ad infinitum, the time to allow time

to take a breath, heaven abandoning us for a long time, yet
in this scene in which the world recreated itself over and
over again, in beauty invented by those who don't have to
answer for it, who are sleeping or away, who will wake up
much later to hear this effusive, delirious, excessive, and yet
sincere tribute, like the rustling of wind through the leaves
or the fuzzy crackling of voices broadcast by machines
invented by a century set on trapping our fever or slowing
down our progress, pushing us towards a detour from our
ancestral paradise, transformed into a modern sky, the
azure as troubling as the future,

those who allow themselves to be surprised and
distracted by the strident, high-pitched song of birds,

those who marvel at the shadows of trees projected
onto dirt roads by the bright intensity of daylight,

those who admire the luxurious life of spring and the
delicacy of newborn green magnified by razor-edged light
at the end of the day,

those who study clouds, believing they can see shapes,
monuments, masterpieces, memories, the outbursts and
moods of their souls emerging from them,

those who worry about the way the sea transforms
things, shifting sand around dunes, acting on devotion and
its heart's delight,

those who mistrust the terrifying power of the sun,
its blinding abundance of light, remembering the sacred
images of figures in ancient worlds who crossed gilt-edged,
white hot clouds in chariots of fire drawn by flaming
horses on the road to a biblical paradise where warrior
kings spoke directly to God without worrying much about
a heaven that didn't yet exist or a hell that was still looking
for a name, demanding that the sun be given back to them
before returning to Earth, drawn by the same indestructible
horses, above armies repenting in gratitude and obedience,

those who bring flowers from their garden,

those who pour bad wine they're proud of,

those who cut bread they've baked themselves,

those who make sure there is water in every glass,
a linen on the table, and food for everyone,

those who softly whisper into the ears of others
translations of conversations in foreign languages they
can't completely grasp,

those who are filled with wonder at the bewitching
candour of children who express their love openly,
awkwardly, and without reserve,

those who recognize the courage you have shown
in your uncompromising desire to tell the truth,

those who return money they've found in the street,

those who are determined to make up for their
mistakes,

those who become impatient with the slow progress
of things,

those who can't grasp the irony of the situation and
who continue on in the generosity bestowed by their good
faith,

those who can no longer find the address to reply to
requests for the details that continue to elude them,

those who correct the bad manners of others because
they have sworn to do so,

those who park on the side of the road to rest for a few
moments, long enough to close their eyes, long enough to
dream that they are flying over a peaceful blue ocean bathed
in serenity, even if it is only for a few minutes,

those who no longer have the strength to keep their
head above water, convinced that they alone are responsible
for the catastrophes, when they have done nothing but tried
in vain to limit the damage,

those who make a spectacle of their greetings, embracing with an excess that shows how pleased they are about the conquests they have witnessed, the desires they have aroused, the passions they have stoked, and, seeing them promptly reciprocated, feel slightly left out, as if everyone were plotting to send them back into the foreign world they had left to be exiled here,

those who tell their life story to perfect strangers,

those who don't scrimp on effort or time to play practical jokes on you,

those who close their ears to the lies of false prophets,

those who go to impossible lengths to ensure that events proceed smoothly and seamlessly,

those who undertake complex operations,

those who drive below the speed limit,

those who look for objects they can give as presents,

those who are tactful, who invent lies,

those who live beyond their means,

those who eat at night without regard for the bad dreams that will disturb their sleep,

those who turn up the volume, sitting behind the steering wheel of cars propelled towards a never-ending list of destinations,

those who talk without stopping, filled with the happiness of finding long-lost friends, who candidly lay out their sorrows and joys, laughing abundantly, tossing their hair nervously, and reconstructing the world with energy and fury, who enjoy themselves and refuse to let the flow of conversation become tepid, who would leave on foot, striding down roads that lead to exile rather than lower their arms, for they have promised to never give up, because to stop talking would be an unforgivable act of weakness, those who have placed their faith in the fresh air, in an irrational belief, taking the time to walk, disguising their raspy breathing and their painful limbs, who promised themselves long ago that it would be better to pay the price than to inflict upon themselves a world becoming putrid, knowing full well that fresh air is a myth and that, whatever anyone does, the world is deteriorating, bowing under the weight of abundance, unable to let go of its all-powerful arrogance which masks a defective life, its worrisome limits, and its deplorable avatars,

those who put up with all kinds of insects, who talk about how badly rain is needed, the good the wind and the cold do, who can read the clemency of the season in the footprints and coats of animals, their night-time obsessions, their constant hunger, and their indecent begging, who stake plants whose stems might collapse, who pluck out weeds, who do battle with the shadows so each can have its rightful portion of sunlight, who have made a pact with the water so that the soil can regenerate, so that paradise can return to Earth in the midst of this sublime tumult that stirs the trees under the wind's influence, their eyes so blue looking from afar over this giddy spectacle, their eyes so blue that heaven can be seen in them as if from the edge of a cliff, their eyes so blue and, in them, a corridor through the centre leading towards the source, when life was nothing more than a distant rumour, take it or leave it, and the sun, slowing the effects of its burning light, consented to all the germs, all the scars that heal more or less quickly, at what price do we still remember, we who are about to breach this pact, we who will leave no worldly inheritance,

those who sit under large leafy trees in the suffocating heat and wait, on an unpretentious and worthless metal throne, for potential customers to arrive,

those who get bored and use their bodies as an object
of amusement to help them cope with the excessive expanse
of their solitude,

those who remember the exact words that made them
laugh, their voices borrowing the inflections, an accent, a
rhythm they carefully mimic, in the hope of producing the
same effect on their audience, which becomes distracted
and perplexed as the performance continues,

those who try desperately to remember what clothes
they were wearing, believing they will find in the pockets
the misplaced words they suddenly and absolutely need to
read,

those who get tired, knowing all too well that the
future will bring them pain that will never leave them in
peace, but who persist all the same, knowing that courage
and endurance will enable them to fly high above, the
entire world as a witness when they land delicately on the
ground and tell everyone they have finally touched heaven,
that they could even have decided to stay there, but they
chose instead to come back to the grave burdens of Earth,
knowing that they can return whenever they please because
now they know the way, knowing that its secret can lodge in
the astonished smiles that they dispense in profusion, a rain
of roses along their path, new saints of a renovated heaven,
their bodies bruised and stretched by their martyrdom, and
having never asked for it, they saw opening before them,
before their unprepared and in fact unwilling eyes, a virtual
paradise of sudden and glorious splendour carried on
the cries of a crowd, which lifted them up to the highest
heavens, close to the false stars, to prolonged applause
that made them forget their promised pain, their bodies
transfigured with fervent beauty,

those who jump as high as they can, hoping to touch
ceilings that are always just beyond their fingertips,
hoping they'll reach them if they try hard enough and
often enough, their bodies exhausted beyond the point of
enduring the repeated leaps towards what eludes them and
the repeated falls that are as predictable as disappointment,

those who carry animals that are too heavy for their
young arms to hold, taking extraordinary care not to
trample on the instinctive sensitivity of these creatures,

those who choose their words carefully in the presence
of grown-ups who listen to their simple requests uttered
with a seductive and astonishing serenity,

those who spend their lives winding up and tinkering
with the explosive device of their anger, plugging it into
the socket of their hard-headedness, waiting for it to power
their custom-designed revenge, a vengeance that will ignite
sparks meant to throw the world off its tracks and force
others to take long detours, turning off the path to a heaven
they hardly care about now but that they saw and watched
and desired so ardently in the past, when they talked about
it in childish whispers that took others aback, imagining
death as a release as easily pictured as eternal deliverance,

those who become annoyed at harsh realities,
wondering how they will get through the rest of their
lives, ceaselessly calculating income, profits, and fortunes,
worrying themselves into a harmful obsessive confusion
that clouds the view of the passage that leads towards
the doorway of escape from the spell that has been cast
over them, the way out of the never-ending labyrinth of
existence,

those who walk faster, pressed on by the rain,
those who bring in the wood for the evening fire,
those who give their time as a gesture of friendship,

those who sleep on beds that are too hard,
those who come back from exhausting travels,
those who profess they are enchanted by the night air,
those who give money to strangers,
those who dream out loud in their sleep,
those who trust in the silence of others,
those who wish for a better world,
those who hold others in their arms in public,
ignoring proper appearances, and who refashion heaven
each time they give in to a gesture so ordinary and yet so
full of wonder,
those who wear themselves out waiting for those
who play the perverse game of making them die of jealousy
and desire, plunging them, at the whim of their fantasies,
faults, and foolishness, into the same hell they have been
struggling to escape, taking refuge in alcohol, work, flesh,
or famine,
those who can't keep up their interest in the world,
preferring a quiet life where silence is a liveable space, a
doorway opening onto a landscape more vast and calm,
a proximate sea the only absolute reference, the solemn
mystery of space spreading out as far as the eye can see,
where the blue floods over the shore, displaying its simple
and steadfast wonders, a future adrift and there, out there
where the blue of the sea merges with the blue of the sky,
imagining a piece of clothing, a cloak white as the cloud's
cover, telling us that paradise is ours, that it will belong
to us when we find a way to turn down the noise, to turn
down our engines long enough to cool, long enough to
leave speech behind, to melt into the vast blue, to become
its surface of memory and the movement of waves, to
find it on the other side, and to see life as a transparent,
unpretentious veil, the vanishing silhouette of an escape as

light and elegant as rain washing away the heavy burdens and troubles of the world, in a place where the sky appears only as a small square of greedy light shaped by a window-frame, catching you by surprise for days and nights, for the precious time you have left to invent plans of escape, to listen in on the bird's secrets of flight and freedom, those who hold back their tears as they think back on the days spent in the same irretrievable place, the youthful euphoria of their arrival and the sudden sadness of their departure,

those who rejoice at the prospect of inviting you soon to their dinner table,

those who thank you for simply being alive, for sharing and breathing the same air, for the gifts that you bring, for something they have glimpsed and felt, like an unforgettable gift, a disaster that radiates unending waves of heat towards them, a new vision that questions and changes everything, that fills them with a giddy complicity, a desire they won't explain and that blankets them in gratitude,

those who quietly take note of your arrival and for whom you suddenly become the only person in sight, who envelop you in their lingering gaze, thinking vaguely about the words they are saying as they calculate your approximate position behind them, the axis on which they are about to turn, shifting with utter delicacy to locate you in their field of vision, in their field of fire, in their field of action, quickly reloading their smiles with exquisite precision, knowing their calibre and range, knowing how to aim and strike the target straight through the heart, straight through the gap that just barely keeps you from a devastating encounter, through the abyss of a heaven they promise you in their arms and with their bodies, in an abyss into which you will sink in spite of your best efforts, if it weren't for all these contradictions to resolve, all these roads to travel, all these smiles to avoid, like so many irresistible ambushes, ice floes drifting into the course you set out for yourself a very long time ago, such a long time ago, and which is now more urgent than ever, a path from which you cannot stray, for heaven will rise before you like the sun, help is on its way, the reason you continually give to justify your resistance will become truth, and, yet, in the promise of these arms, there also lies a hint, a breath of salvation that returns like a smile borrowed or perhaps stolen from angels, a ray of light that takes you by the hand, pushes you ahead, enfolds you in its arms, opens your eyes, for the road to heaven is a river that flows quietly around the whirlpools of everyday existence, and no doubt we should follow its slow and slothful meanderings, its inevitable wastes, and experience the astonishing and wondrous magic spell it casts, but instead you turn your head and smile without extravagance, modestly, as a matter of form, for the simple, glorious fact that you, too, are alive, and you turn to other matters, to your numerous distractions, to other smiles, to other bodies, to other gazes, and the angel slips away, discreetly taking away the tenderness of the instant when the night would finally open up for you to make dreams, to create a fragile yet durable grace, when heaven suddenly returns to your memory and the world takes shape as a fading copy, a vast, expanding temptation, the devil borrowing an angel's eyes, lips, and voice, making you tremble on the cliff's edge of that look, the moment when words slip off key and become distorted in an unfamiliar scale, for heaven is mute, even when the night extends its promises under the glow of desire, heaven holds its tongue under the serene influence of a recalled thought that wanders off again and fades in the memory of a night that blocks off its avenues, of a slumber that returns in peaks of forgetfulness and wonder, of dreams that reach towards the limits of the night where you finally let yourself slide, your head resting on the moon, your body sprinkled with stars, your eyes barely open, letting in, through the sublime crack, a stroke of blue, intangible proof of heaven's defeat and return, of a presence that inhabits each of us with hope clutched like a trophy because you have crossed the wasteland and now you swim in the waters of a river where your body comes back to life eternally, delivered from its torments, filled with tenderness under the protection of a peace that will pass the test of time, those who gaze absent-mindedly through the window, waiting for a sign that their solitude is about to end,

those who accept their disappointments with patience as they wait in the river for fish that never come,

those who sound out noises to make up for the vocabulary they lack,

those who speak to you under the cover of silence and complicity, believing that intimacy, solidarity, and compassion can grow out of the secrecy of a shared misfortune,

those who kneel beside your chair to put themselves at eye level,

those who make plans for the future,

those who bend under the weight of illusion,

those who are disarming in their sincerity,

those who lick their wounds,

those who try to understand the awkward and surprising gestures of love,

those who fly kites,

those whose balloons float away into the horizon,

those who have made their lives into a puzzle that can never be put together,

those who return at nightfall, their bodies heavy with the daily weight of disproportionate effort,

those who stand by and casually watch as important papers are blown away by ferocious gusts of wind as unexpected as they are uncontrollable,

those who make sure that beauty will always sustain the subtle and impeccable arrangement in which the world can regain its balance and life its moving complicity,

those who clean up and give everything away,

those who face inescapable disorder,

those who complain about the fickle ways of those

who no longer know how to recognize the value of work
and devotion, but who perform once again, for their benefit,
with the same generosity, and the same gestures, never
noticing the delicate intentions nor the suppressed rage nor
even the bitter smile,

> those who give away their books,

> those who pay for the wine, just to be polite,

> those who leave enormous tips,

> those who give up the limelight and take their seats in
the shadows,

> those who drink straight out of the bottle,

> those who are outraged by the constant, widespread
existence of lies both tolerated and rewarded,

> those who walk slowly, absorbing the landscape, who
pay attention to the most common things, rediscovering life
in its inexhaustible inventiveness, and its inborn sense of
continuity, who give thanks for the splendour found in the
simplest places and the most ordinary moments, who give
thanks for colour, for the rain, for birdsong, for leaves, for
the heaven they have brought down to Earth and through
which they move slowly and surely, delivered from the
present, placed back in the world, and, beyond the world,
this ordinary and majestic life, carrying with care down
roads rich with wonder the book of a splendid life that they
will never write,

> those who lift up gigantic stones that they believe are
teeming with life so intense and thought-provoking that it
makes them dizzy for the rest of their days,

> those who pick out fruit, poking it to see if it is firm
enough, and serve it to those for whom they have affection,

> those who venture towards the sea and double back,
distressed by the sight of odd and worrisome creatures
crawling on the sand,

those who plan meetings,
those who make others comfortable,
those who ask after you,
those who write down addresses,
those who take pictures,
those who trot out their memories,
those who read their love letters over again,
those who put their bandages back on,
those who sing along with the radio,
those who open the mail,
those who take out the garbage,
those who go back over their steps,
those who get their children dressed,
those who have given up on eternal youth,
those who tie back their hair,
those who lose weight,
those who make babies,
those who drive trucks,
those who sleep under the stars,
those who recycle garbage,
those who serve drinks,
those who buy wholesale,
those who write love letters,
those who make clothes,
those who water plants,
those who drink in secret,
those who keep their doors closed,
those who make up for lost time,
those who follow a schedule,
those who are still undecided,
those who change their minds,
those who smoke at night,
those who give out their number,

those who laugh on the phone,
those whose money burns a hole in their pocket,
those who kiss children,
those who grind their teeth,
those who make funny faces so others will laugh,
those who step down,
those who dry their own tears,
those who fear the worst,
those who bend over backwards,
those who live in the here and now,
those who have the last word,
those who get right to the heart of the matter,
those who listen to the same record again and again,
those who get a kick out of your mistakes,
those who take as long as they need,
those whose heart is in the right place,
those who lie back with their eyes closed,
those who borrow money,
those who fret over the misfortune of others,
those who keep food past the expiry date,
those who rescue insects,
those who refuse to eat the flesh of animals,
those who rule the roost,
those who glow with happiness,
those who transplant trees,
those who bring plants back to life,
those who feed flowers,
those who keep their promises,
those who understand without knowing,
those who believe in goodness,
those who want peace and nothing more,
those who say what needs to be said,
those who have the courage to continue,

those who have the right to know,
those who feel like dropping everything,
those who need reassurance,
those who harbour deep sadness and private tragedy,
those who decide otherwise,
those who have enough love for two,
those who love so much their hearts break,
those who love without hope,
those who love beyond reason and beyond strength,
those who love beyond the limits of love,
those who love and will love for a long time yet,
those who love all life long,
those who love without end,
those who love for the pleasure of loving,
those who love without keeping track,
those who love without really wanting to,
those who love and adore you,
those who love and worry,
those who love and despair,
those who live on love,
those who love the scent of your skin,
those who love 'til they're raw with pain,
those who love from the depths of their inner beings,
those who love the shape of your lips,
those who love the sound of your voice,
those who love when they could hate instead,
those who love and know how it will end,
those who love despite the obstacles,
those who love despite the distance,
those who love extravagantly,
those who love excessively,
those who love ecstatically,
those who love absolutely and to utter abandon,

those who love because love is included in the price
of heaven, a preview on Earth of this global and essential
fusion that unites and enchants us, the renunciation of our
body, denied, opening itself, which is happiness, you might
say, our continuous and painless surrender to a state in
which the smallest element of existence is magnified into
an astonishing silhouette of emotion finally and fully alive
in the translucent abundance of a place made ever more
beautiful by the euphoria of being alive, of being in love, of
being in heaven,

those who try to chase away from their minds the
attempts to which they subject themselves to save face,
to pretend that life is simpler than it seems, and to repeat
this simple and obvious conclusion to themselves, like
the promise of a white winter they will spend trying to
distance themselves from bad memories as they stumble
through the snow, their heart heavy and cold with sorrow,
wrapped in a cumbersome coat like a solid monument to
suffering, bravely enduring the stubborn pace that leads
them away from warmth, a place left to them from their
earliest childhood, a place they will never reach, a love
they've forgotten under the snow that will return to them,
that must return, they are utterly aware of it, their certainty
extreme and durable, built up under a snow so light, but for
the time being, they simply move forward, their steps so
long, so slow, so heavy that they lose themselves in clothes
that are too old, too big, too huge in the portrait of the
sorrow that they carry, never realizing that they will carry
it all their lives, that it is a spell cast in stone too heavy to
evacuate and which will follow them, as the avenging angel
of destiny leads them to one misfortune after another and,
finally, to the ultimate destiny towards which they head
with courage and conviction on the foggy road they travel,
moving through a troubled world, on the path to heaven,
the inexhaustible space, the buoy tossed on the turbulent
seas of sorrow, the invisible beacon of nights abandoned in
patience and solitude, the unfulfilled promise that left them,
in exchange, this will, this tension, this struggle for a better
world, a place of rest that they clearly seem determined
to desire and avoid, the pervasive contradiction of their
lives, earning their place in heaven in the customary way,
with each step becoming a dangerous undertaking and
each heartbeat an unfathomable plunge, pacing out the

huge distance that separates us from the stars, the place
of compromise where it will finally become possible to
measure the interstellar distance that separates us from
paradise, an unchanging place of reward waiting for us after
our compulsory journey along the path laid out before us,

those who refuse to renounce the faith they cobbled
together when, as small children, they could already
glimpse the profile of a world built to the dimensions of
their overflowing imaginations, the same place where
the unconscious traces were born of dreams infused with
mystery and magic, the release of fears accumulated since
childhood and even beyond in the obscure labyrinths where
space is regenerated, where they grew up, protected from
themselves in the shadow of those who wished them ill,

those who write, looking for the right word, leafing
through the dictionary of memories to give faith to the
distress that perches on their shoulder, telling them to
surrender, telling them that they are the product and victim
of a huge deception and that words will flee from their lips
and disappear forever, "you shall die silent" repeated ad
nauseam above their heads and outlined in the halo of an
infamous distress that sneaks into their daily struggle to put
confidences on paper, to steal speech and cries for help, and
to fly over the world with a panoramic view of the promised
land, where they see assembled grace and the deluge of a life
whose meaning slips through their fingers and cannot be
held, and, yet, is ever-present, more grave and astonishing
than these words, which will never manage to contain it
well or truly,

those who err on the side of confidence, having found
inside themselves the limitless generosity that inspires great
passions and draws you towards exceptional beings, lending
them your spirit to sustain their travels, opening your heart
to engulf their lives of beauty, confiding in them the secrets
of your soul to inspire their careless lives, giving them your
body to lighten the weight of their solitude, beings who
will one day transform themselves into spectres of your
loss, vampires who will haul you back to the bosom of their

hell, as if this passage could raise the dead, as if the ashes of these flames could still strike fear into the heart, for you whose world is untouchable and whose desire will always be renewed by another bout of excessive confidence that will carry you far beyond the living and the dead, far above those who believed they saw past your quavering, who believed they heard your cry echoing through the labyrinths of distress, for such generosity runs the risk of confusing those whose myopic confidence associates life with a conspiracy and resignation with a spell cast by ambitious and mysterious forces,

those who have seen death grip them in the tentacles of a thunderous highway, when all they wanted was to hear the bone-tired lament of beggars, the outrageous burden that, without the benefit of grace which used to be so necessary, abandons us to the spinning concentric circles of damnation, with strange creatures and cruel machines, where heaven takes on the garb of a phony and fickle rumour and would, at first glance, be seen as an illusion, if it weren't for the constant and omnipresent glow, the half-light, the luminous presence crossing the dust to claim us and take us away to a far-off place where confusion runs the risk of becoming a way of life, oh, but to place this weight upon the ground and to see rising up from it the light, translucent sheath covering the blue of the sky, what better project could we design to exact our deliverance, we, who have driven from such distances and walked for so long to bear witness, with our eyes filled with bitterness, to a miracle so startling, to a future so unique, those who have recreated the universe and invented, often without knowing, a world where rebellion is sent under the innocuous cover of drawing breath, a way of making the present detour towards the future, their vigilance following the contours of the face of virtue, their voices floating above a disproportionate vision, listening to a vast and vigorous refrain, a song escaping in spite of itself from their memory and their lips, a hymn to life, to the tides that carry them away from unwanted shores, from the green villages they evacuated, where they sometimes dream of returning to live,

those who read cards, believing they've found the hands of fate in the awkward tones of a voice turning into a lament and a persistent anguish, pushing away catastrophe and rebuilding success on the spot, so that the sun of solitude is transformed into a love song, trying to negotiate the ultimate merger of a heavy, cold pride and a hope that continues to reinvent itself in gardens of endlessly blooming flowers, in night eyes staring at the blue body of the moon until it disappears into the periphery, crosses enchanted forests, slides through wells of light, or consumes its reflection in the pool with the eyes of love, where heaven hides nothing more than an eternal complacency, while you cut yourself and make a wish that the world would slip through your fingers, gripping the emptiness of another adventure, the obsessive silence of a cry for help that can barely be heard, the messages that can no longer be transmitted, the outdated prophecy that continues to make promises, those who sleep in carriages, embarking on a life that already hints of unending noise and unclear feelings, who curl up in flannelette, clutching with newborn hands the tiny comforts, the happiness that submerges space when it appears in all its mystifying splendour, the tranquil, delicate slumber under the sand sprinkled on their eyelids, the smiles they provoke and the long detour they are about to take, drifting with majestic slowness on the tiny raft of their life, the little patch of heaven, pure and luminous, that they carry with them, clutching it in their clenched fists, still vaguely remembering the milky destiny to which they cling in their embryonic dreams, aware that they must carry it back, intact and enlarged, convinced that they will have to sew from its cloth a sparkling, starlit ultramarine coat, when at last they find themselves before the open gate of return, which they presume exists and towards which they travel, those whose light breath already knows the secret of all the nights, all the possibilities held in the gentle breathing that barely lifts the cotton veil tenderly placed on top of them, tucking them in, and shielding them delicately from the destinies of others, waiting patiently in the courtyard before a heaven they momentarily abandoned to become the living proof of its existence, those who live under the nightmare thumbs of those whose murderous intentions and triumphant disdain once made them celebrants of an exalted and excessive hatred, posing as tenants of an unspeakable sorrow transformed into a vengeance towards anything weak and confused that life can produce, an exaggerated and excessive sorrow displayed at every occasion, without regard for restraint, civility, or even simple decency, a hate as large as human desire for all that is troubled or submissive, a hate so much like anguish, circulating at night in the sleep of those whose smile was once tinged with forgiveness, with the salvation of resignation, and who are now loathed for being so generous with their beauty, so tolerant in their outlandish understanding, so striking, so radiant, so alive, and whom they have sworn to make into victims, casting into their world dreadful curses and enraged, coiling serpents that strangle innocent and harmless trees,

those who wonder how to dampen the flames that consume them with desire, a god to whom they have sacrificed their second-hand dignity, the nearly anonymous hands that fondle them as they pass by, making their precious gems dazzle until they finally can just not believe in all that glitters, a god envying the fragile beauty they have constructed from scratch, begging them for a vaccine against time and its ravages, promising to grant them, in return, a glory as overstated as it is short-lived, that can no longer be revived, time, as a venom against nature whose remedy will be found between the legs where eternal youth still burns, where transfixing dreams are transacted, where disturbing viruses are planned under the influence of unmanageable flames where the world is perpetually embroiled, where hell in all its excess takes up occupancy, where the luminescent blue of heaven is obscured by a

screen rolled down before the fires of hell, the embers that
burn for eternity, consuming the living in the obscure
ravages wreaked by hell,

      those who calculate the way they will be riddled with
poison before devouring their breath, who have experienced
the sly manipulations of love, its cruel games, when the
devil puts on his evening cloak and stealthily discusses the
state of the world, speaking openly to people who virtuously
suck out poison, their love taking on the appearance of a
wondrous illness, the most gentle and powerful of antidotes,
injected directly into the eyes, ears, and mouth before
invading the distant forest whose perfume spreads like a
troubling fog, the tremor that sometimes anchors the Earth,
that swells the omnipotent heaven with pride, that time uses
to measure the scope of deceit, that is emptied into the river
and about to take your breath away, the body dumbfounded,
as if heaven could still throw itself eternally under the
wheels of a desire that revs up as the devil creeps away at
dawn, after having danced all night long, abandoning the
world on its unmade bed, covered in bite-marks, and ready
to die laughing, clutching in clenched fists the sheets where
life rediscovers its momentum and heads for heaven,

      those who, without flinching, watch their world fall
apart, their voices echoing the deception they are trying
with all their might to contain, their every gesture measured
with care as everything slips away around them and
threatens to alter their tranquil, serene, diligently cultivated
landscape, filling the wastelands in the blink of an eye with
memories retrieved as well as could be expected from the
smoky, nostalgia-tinted ruins they will continue to visit
until the end of time,

      those who have seen their beauty sink into the well of
fatigue, searching everywhere for precise reasons to justify

the proof of their labour, blowing on their faces to set off miniature hurricanes that once gave them the elegance and charm they emitted as if they were God's gift to the world, the disturbing confidence of time which is already ravaging their hands and spreading to their faces, their fading smiles, their constant effort to contain the world in a state of weightlessness in their eyes, to tell their invisible, life-changing truths with disconcerting nonchalance, and to continue to turn heads, whatever anyone might say,

those who embody places, times, and functions, who raise tides of desire in their wake as they move cautiously through the world, check up on the way things are going, and mechanically consult obscure chronicles, greying documents, boring files, who will never say anything without insisting on putting things back in place after taking pleasure in shifting the same objects by minuscule incisions that perforate the membrane of time, the harmless gestures of a body changing places, the enchanted gaze of a refreshed universe, the endless motion of extending a hand, the sublime slow crossing of legs, parting of lips, closing of eyes, or shifting of a body, leaning gently on the indestructible solidity of grey metal furniture when desire slips out of its clamp, surges up like the eternal fountain of time snuggling up under the eyelids, the well you long to drink from blocked by a smile tucked into a voice that mumbles small talk,

those whose bodies awkwardly take on the shape of life and whose round contours encase the mysteries of the world, the return through anger vigorously affirming life's continuity, perforating it, leaving it something of itself which, if it is not submission, can at least make subversive use of it, plunging it deep into water and exhibiting it like the unimaginable membrane of a star when night falls,

burning, gluing sand and rage together, plunging deep into
saliva, inventing new visions and turning away black kohl
eyes so that the sea will come and engulf life, come and lose
itself in life, stealing its blue origins before disappearing
quickly into the infinite blue to melt into the blue of
heaven, perhaps giving itself over to life as it did in the
past, before the emergence of shapes hereafter imbued with
heavy shudders, in a perpetual enigma tested as far back
as childhood, the mystery of an end that was then nothing
more than the acquired rights and the inevitable admission
that this azure would finally be found, like an indescribable
continent whose mystery excites and provokes, sinking,
losing itself, and dissoving into the blue of heaven at last,

      those who ask children to dance with them, taking
them by the hand, making allowances for their clumsiness,
for their slowness, for their awkward need to be part of
the dance, to see how grand it is and how far it will go
when the real dance comes and takes them away for good,
consuming them body and soul, fitting them into unknown
destinies and exorcising the urge to live that has been with
them since childhood, the childhood where they move
awkwardly for the moment, gripping onto the rough and
reassuring hand of the woman who compliments them
profusely on their modest efforts, enjoying the laughter that
punctuates the rhythm, their own, on which they lean with
absolute confidence so they won't fall or lose face, so they'll
be able to set off on the road that feels already like an arena,
a springboard, a mirror barely touching the face at the cost
of a lightness that makes you want to spin around high and
far until the world is nothing more than a misty, sublime
illusion, distant and hazy, a stirring of the heart that lifts you
up until heaven appears as a mirage that can be reached, a
joy that can be fulfilled, a refuge, a hall where people dance

with their faces against the countenance of the universe, a
celestial scent suddenly rising up from the wandering paths
of the Earth, a call to come up close enough for our hearts
to beat in the same rhythm, our bodies swaying like the
flowers dancing on their stems or spinning in the awkward
circle where someone holds your hand, murmurs to you
that you are doing well, that you are doing very well, that
it's good, and where no one can burst the fragile membrane
upon which you are rising to the clouds and even above
them, where all life is manifest, and where dance so
intensely resembles the felicitous, light-hearted, wholesome
deliverance that, in other times and perhaps forever, has
released the idea of salvation, such an old plan, a rather
old-fashioned idea to give meaning back to a floundering
life, to music, to dance in the steps of a body moving in time
to a tireless allegro, to the beat of music muffled by nearby
yet unpredictable rumours of a paradise lost and yet so
absolutely necessary,

those who lose themselves in the manners of an earlier
era, dreaming they've escaped from stifling, overheated
workplaces,

those who remove their clothes and walk slowly into
the sea, carefully taming the cold claws of the water,

those who never see the sun, who are obliged to shut
themselves off, and serve as wardens of dreams others have
dreamed for them,

those who grow impatient at the thought of being
tossed around by the blue of the waves reminiscent of the
indelible, unending blue afternoons of their childhood,

those who sit and read under the cover of parasols,
not worrying about the kiss of death the sun is preparing
to place upon their carefree bodies, carried away by the
magic of words,

those who repeatedly stroke their bodies, trying to
keep from being bitten by the unwelcome, persistent insects
flying in circles over their naked, delicious, and vulnerable
skin,

those who flap at the dust suspended in the heat,
obedient to the slightest gesture or draught, before falling to
Earth in an abominable veil of dirt that sinks to the ground,

those who replace others who take off for a rest and
leave them to shudder and suffocate under the pale cold
fanned through their deserted offices,

those who take baths to get rid of the heat seeping
into their bodies, dreading the idea of long, wakeful nights,

those who stare aimlessly as heat works its way across
a ravaged landscape in the middle of a summer when snow
is only an unreliable memory,

those who hold their tongues, mindful that they no
longer have the time to do everything that used to make
them happy,

those who admire the playful beauty of light, its fragile and fleeting reflections, its talent to thread through the shadows and make the green of the forest glow,

those who fall asleep on the floor during heat waves, dreaming they have climbed a mountain higher than the sky, hoping they will never have to come back down,

those who walk with great care through improbable
yet necessary locations,

those who turn around, intrigued by the way
unfamiliar music has fulfilled its promise,

those who are resilient to insults, absorbed in their
work and in the patience of their detachment,

those who have stored up their reserves of motherly
love for children they've never borne,

those who have run out of excuses and reached the
disappointing limits of their abilities,

those who let you know about implausible ills that
are sure to befall you and the exact effect and extent of the
ravages these scourges will cause,

those who write sincere and affectionate words to
conjure up the sad fortunes that those who are leaving will
probably encounter,

those who prepare extravagant meals to make up for
neglect or a slight, of which they are the unwilling victims,

those who are upset by the risks you've taken in
undertaking tasks they consider dangerous,

those whose trail is a stream of light so brilliant that it
seems as if they have forgotten to close heaven's door,

those who work on their hands and knees,
those who avoid the callous judgment of mirrors,
those who always eat the same food,
those who make sure their surroundings look nice,
those who write letters and receive no replies,
those who doubt the universe is worthy,
those who yank at their skirts to make them look
longer,
those who want the world to suit their fancy,
those who weep in childlike distress,
those who believe that paradise is already on Earth,
those who plod from one sleepless night to the next,
ignoring the frenzy of life careering to its end, swallowing
massive doses of sleeping pills and never finding sleep
or even rest, knowing it only from the heavy books they
pore over, reading the same advice over and over again,
the advice that continues to have no effect whatsoever on
the fate in which they are trapped, not wanting to have
anything to do with cries, blows, or costly kisses, having
long ago decided to plunge into the silence of their lives,
who have made a vow of perpetual awakening, unique and
tireless beings who lean on the night without counting on
it, without ever muttering a reproach, who give up dreams
to live with their eyes wide open, damming up the tidal
sobs that get stuck in their throat, declaring war on their
suffering, their misery, and their boredom, wondering what
life could possibly have in store for them other than the
heaven they once were given at their birth, the poison apple
of boundless patience, the gift of vigilance that everyone
envies, comparing them to angels of peace who gave the
coats off their backs to those who were cold, their food to
those who watched them eat, and their hearts to those who
had none, who looked up to the sky from which they have

trouble flying away, their confusing world gluing them to
the sheets on which they are sitting, getting used to the idea
that heaven belongs to those who have managed to avoid
hell, but how can they describe this, how can they tell their
story other than to stare endlessly, transfixed by the little
patch of light that grows more intensely blue with every day
that passes, a map on which the world traces a blurry path,
repositioning itself in the same halo, along the same road,
and at the same place and time, giving them a life force, an
energy that surges from their guts, and a faith that sustains
their belief that dreams might come true when one has lived
in heaven long enough, without knowing much about it
and without living there, never considering how it is
possible to close one's eyes in the middle of the day, in the
brightest midnight when birds fall asleep, how it is possible
to retrace the world's path on the lost map, the scrap of a
half-lived life, the starlit sky which, from an unimaginable
distance, makes paradise appear probable and perplexing,

those who know the lyrics of songs by heart and
who raise their voices in places where they once tasted the
pleasure of feeling the wind stick its head under the door to
convince them that they were in charge of their own space,
that it would never get warm and that summer, like love,
was simply a mirage invented by those who played music
the way others talk about hell and high water, who found
in songs a hazy universe and a manageable way to position
their bodies in the wind so they wouldn't be carried away by
its acts, its body, and its cries and so that they wouldn't have
to negotiate with the devastating gusts to keep up the voice
and the music which, like the heart, is incapable of lying,

those who improvise little dance steps that they insert
like stakes in your gaze, like vectors in your movements,
like needles in your distractions, slyly laying claim to their
territory, designing a shelter for the future far beyond the
smiles into which you are sliding, totally unaware, the
sidelong glances with which they betray themselves and
the lascivious poses they strike, ignoring the consequences,
the duration, and the frequency, let alone the irreparable
damage they could cause,

those who empty their closets to find a suitable outfit,
something that will do the trick, do the job, make the day,
make the deal, something that will cut through banality
and give them a silky-smooth elegance in which skin rises
back to the surface of daylight like a bouquet of roses
with a compelling perfume, placing their lips against the
delicate soft fabric, black straps cutting into pale, naked
shoulders, who return empty-handed, having missed the
target of their desire, forgetting promises they've made to
put an end to this scarcity, laying down such predictable
disappointments between cold white sheets, the bed like a
raft cast improbably adrift, and who wander into the black

and trembling night towards heaven, with only a vague idea
of where to go, forgetting how far, which way, and why they
are wandering around, and wondering, as always, which
outfit they should have worn to have the desired effect once
they got to wherever it was they were going,

     those who have flowers inscribed on their skin,
imagining an entire garden in the point of the needle whose
ink and pain they welcomed like sun on fertile soil, smiling
comfortably at the distant sight of those who will be thrilled
by the indigo garden injected into the lines of golden skin
that swells under the breeze of breath, engorged with
sweat and flowing with abundance, a light, delicate rain
lighting on the eyelids, blurring the vision of those who,
incredulous, watch the garden doors open wide, the night's
mystery revealed by the secret flower whose rare and distant
poison leads people into the temptation of an ecstasy that
they suspect will create in their soul a wish, a longing for
heaven, that will last their whole life long,

     those who leave the scene of the drama, the corridors
infused with the folly of their youth, when they took
themselves for great ladies and now talk in an offhand way
about the last days of those who crossed the desert to stand
beside them at the gates of death, considering themselves
rebellious by the very idea of producing such a substantial
inventory of memories, imagining themselves called by
some sort of mission, and alluding to the death from which
others have not returned and who, having climbed over
the wall of great discord too early in their lives, have stayed
there, unable to resign themselves to any true departure,
poisoning the lives of the living, chilling them with panic in
the middle of long, boozy nights spent trying to build fences
around the abyss, chasing them through the mazes of fear,
hurling insults upon obscenities upon threats, admitting to

their attempts to delay the ultimate end and leaving anyway and anyhow, hands gripping the door about to close forever against the cascade of laughter, the anecdotes, the laconic comments about having to live until you die, until heaven proves its existence, showing up as a clearing, a river, or whatever else it might become, those who see life as a cross to bear,

those who hear the music of the breezes,

those who take the time to walk,

those who have food brought in,

those who tell themselves that life is a gift,

those who look after other people's children,

those who put up with shows of manliness,

those who laugh at their own stories,

those who make sure the room is quiet so that others
can sleep,

those who are unsure of what they know,

those who spread the energy of despair,

those who believe in the beauty of the universe,

those who talk about happier days,

those who switch from one language to another,

those who catch you off guard with their charm,

those who share their happiness by repeating its
sudden miracle,

those who consider themselves blessed by life,

those who are worthy of the heaven of their childhood,

those who lie on their side on wooden benches to
counter the pain that sears through their muscles, forgetting
nothing from the past in which they threw themselves
into space in a state of sublime weightlessness, hung from
delicate threads of light from which their safety nets and
clothing were woven, a body whose thin anonymity has
transformed over time into a single majestic smile, who
tell you, in spite of themselves, that memory is the seat
of emotion, an unconquerable fortress, a moment in the
depths of a valley, the emptiness of a Saturday evening when
it is getting cold outside and when time doesn't know how
to do anything but spend itself taking other lives, sometimes
lifting them up to the sky, the terminal at the end of a
mandatory, conscientious pilgrimage, measuring icy
glances and navigating troubled waters under the influence
of suffering that burns at the slightest provocation, and then
to arrive at the heaven that humans could easily believe was
lost forever, were it not for the hard wooden bench that
keeps pushing your back into spasms of pain, letting you
meditate on the place where all ill fortune is erased and
where angels never needed wings to fly, to the point where
your eyes must have forgotten their presence,

those who shoot up, loading their needles to
compensate for all they have never had, who trade in
one misery for another, who are trapped in a damp,
drafty hollow, who have taken root with rage and fury in
the depths of their own selves, stretching down like a tree
with roots throbbing and overgrown, their despair met with
the reward of a promise equal to coming back to life, a bad
debt settled whose returns are irritating and worrying, the
rivers of blood they can imagine irrigating veins swollen
with pride and pain at the thought that heaven might return
to Earth, that the child will be strong and gentle, that he
will look upon our old world with new and healing eyes,
that life will merge with life and destiny will flow with it
towards the mouth of heaven, towards whatever is left of
our dreams, hopes, and illusions, that there will at least be
enough to cope with the syringes that prick and sting the
skin on an autumn night when leaves are preparing for their
long, painful separation from branches that have watched
them bud and grow green in the ecstatic rustling of prayers
brightly tinted with their long, conclusive fatigue,

those who do impressions, modulating their voices
to the tones of those they've known and whose vibrating
sounds they can remember, indulging in their accents,
which they casually exaggerate, bringing along with their
voice a space, a discomfort, a position, and a judgment
that takes form mindlessly, knowing that laughter delivers
us from the evil errors of existence and that the real world
exists, no doubt, in some other place, in the laughter rising
up out of nowhere tonight, like a fragile, flickering flame
lighting up an unexpected space with a courageous, new
warmth before it turns into a blinding blaze whose light
forms the radiant firmament of our dreams,

those who wait for the right time to activate their
innate sense of humour, who are on the lookout for things
to laugh at, who are ready to let themselves be shaken with
the delighted shudders their bodies have contained since
the day they were born, who are unable to predict where,
when, or who will contribute to making this laughter spill
out and spread through their surroundings, tumbling out
like tiny multicoloured stones, toppling like the vibrations
of delirious vocal cords, laying themselves out in the sun
like the cool, calm serenity of soundtracks on which
eardrums will record glee as memorable as love and as
deadly as ridicule, the bitter laughter for which they will
always be the remedy, the potent, if not fatal, cure, and who
really should know by now, those who take their seats on
hard, cold chairs and wait patiently while the world comes
back to life in a mysterious and transitory setting, where
music sounds like a devilish and playful rhythm coursing
through crowds of passersby who occasionally stop to listen
absent-mindedly to the litany, before starting on their way
again, shaking their heads, impervious to the falling night,

those who show curious children unusual objects, calling them over to see the beauty and miracles, attracting their wandering attention to the colour, the luxurious textures, the dancing reflections of sparkling surfaces, the intricate arrangements, and who adjust their voices to tune into a sense of wonder that takes their breath away and gives rise to joy,

those who put nurslings to sleep, cuddling those who can't help but fall into sleep, their desperate cries echoing through the dusk until they fade into the sound of waves, into the unclouded paths of light traced by the sparks that escape from campfires and zigzag blindly through heavy, opaque nights, their haunted paths tracing strange warnings, calls for help, piercing shouts of anger,

those who predict the end of the world, relying on their infallible interpretations of sacred texts passed down from worlds long gone, who don't notice that, in their cigarette smoke, fragile and vaporous words are spelling out prophecies just as trustworthy and relevant, and who are content to look once again over the traces left on smudged pages by those who have gone before and recorded their catastrophic visions that still lurk in the recesses of our minds,

those plunged by sudden luck into a state of confusion from which they can emerge glorious, destined to start their life all over again on a continent where affection is common currency, the abundant hope of children who confide in you the secrets of their souls, with certainty that you will transform them in dreams, laughter, and patience with visions still taking form,

those who water plants, finding in this simple morning ritual a reconciliation unlike any other, marvelling at the green mystery of life which recomposes a universe from a simple seed, serving as guardians of paradise and letting themselves be led, under the clothing that imprisons them in modern customs, towards a splash of colour, a carefree pleasure, an everlasting garden of heaven formed in their image and in their likeness and out of which they were once so cruelly and unfairly chased, forced into the senseless and unfeeling desert, those who are amused by the determined efforts of animals that go through garbage in search of food,

those who are amazed at signs of intelligence, even in its most humble form,

those who learn how to operate complex, dangerous, and powerful tools,

those who watch absent-mindedly as crazy and delightful projects develop under their eyes,

those who lose patience, who are unable to stand by and watch so much capricious deceit,

those who wake up, overwhelmed by the number and urgency of jobs to be done,

those who dissolve into tears, as though the world's suffering had suddenly penetrated them,

those who take courage by remembering days gone by when they were in love,

those who go over their tracks to find out what details attracted them in the first place,

those who can't manage to pull themselves out of the bitterness they have used to build a prison around them,

those who talk about how fascinating the human body is, even in its most humble and ordinary motions,

those who work, as the only woman among men, sharing the same hard, weary lives,

those who cry out at the sight of beautiful objects that charm and bewitch them,

those who are determined to prove that time has stolen something from them and that it can never be replaced,

those who can't afford to be led into risky, dead-end situations,

those who hold their breath to stifle the despair they can't express, those who tell long-winded stories about the memorable moments of their childhood,

those who whisper into your ear that they worry about disappearing into the eyes of others,

those who point out the unforgettable places where their life suddenly came to a halt,

those who can no longer share their beauty with the world because they are terrorized by the reflections of mirrors,

those who pack their bags again, anticipating their flight to heaven, certain they will be lifted there at last,

those who have broken their contract with death and
re-established their complete confidence in the power of
love to act as an antidote to the pain raging through their
lives, reviving the moments during which the world beyond
this one seemed to move towards them, the moment when
passion promises miracles upon miracles and which will
vanish under the delirious glow of the sun, the blazing fire
they lit themselves so far away and so long ago, in a village
shaken by wind and misery, their posthumous glory now
useless, listed occasionally in a back-page column of the
newspaper, their value now worthless in the bland suffering
offered to feed the multitudes, the story we circulate like
gossip, in airplanes that rush back to the scene of the crime,
the destination of a sad journey, the tears that pour out, a
face streaming with powerless sorrow, and a world sorely
lacking in the sight of the throbbing spectacle and the music
that goes on and on, that must go on at all costs, that goes
on by itself, as heaven is nothing more than a distant echo
populated with doubts and truths, unfathomable except in
anger, and a confession made that love may settle into its own
home, so that my road may be the final destination of all my
prayers, so that my life should stumble along until I draw
my last breath, so that my last word should be the name of
the strange and necessary love that resembles the paradise
we contemplate in our imaginings, the heaven where we
shall find those we love and others whose mistrust, insults,
and mean-spiritedness we will have already forgiven, where
we shall at last gather them around us,

    those who can't find the words to describe their
embarrassment when asked to give the real reason which
led them to act in such an inexplicable manner, who
withdraw quietly into a silence that can't be translated into
the language they have invented to compensate for words

that don't exist, words as unimaginable as undiscovered
continents, and who have chosen to go through the motions
of an awkward series of half-smiles, uncomfortable, graceless
postures, stressful moments when it seems as if they are
victims of a heart attack, an unbearable languishing in
the dreary rain when there is no one anywhere to fill the
emptiness, where there is only the rage, the sighs, a manner
of staring far off towards a still invisible place where it would
be so good to be, longing only to move towards that place,
to seek refuge there, to settle there, to escape from this
airless, suffocating trap,

 those who turn around, conquered by the tender
presence of love approaching them, conscious of the side
effects produced by such ploys, the feelings they have
trouble describing in words, fleeing at the hint of a threat
and taking refuge in the labyrinths of modern buildings,
holding in their trembling hands the thread that will help
them find the door to the formless sound of a cash register,
the desperate flight where happiness becomes the panting
monster chasing them through nightmares, groaning and
moaning, the injured beast collapsing against a cement wall,
in the tragic and irreparable beam of a light that spreads
over the ground,

 those who steadfastly write their life story on clay
tablets, while all around them people dwell on their slightest
confidences, dissecting them and hiding in the pink flesh
of their lips the signs of a disdain that once harboured an
irresistible charm, contorting in the discomfort they seemed
resigned to bear, their legs knotted around their towering
chairs, bonded to their clay tablets, about to absorb their
secret disappointments, while elsewhere people endlessly
proclaim declarations of their misguided intentions, their
trivial moments of raised consciousness, their thoughtless

indignations, their meaningless confessions, or their
foreseeable conclusions,

those who go out for air, suffocating in rooms where
the sun has taken up residence, leaning up against the
cool, rough edges of rocks, folding their legs in the grips of
their encircling arms, waiting until the air freshens before
returning to their earnest and urgent tasks, the discreet
and well thought-out speech that constantly returns to the
question of underlying, inadmissible nostalgia, the memory,
the commemoration of a storm that has developed into
a melancholy tale, a summer that will end up ending, an
autumn about to begin, and a winter over the horizon that
can't be avoided, like the ice where they once stretched out
for a moment to cool the twin flames of the fire that will
consume them,

those who set the table, making sure that life remains
a simple, full, wholesome gift made in the image of meals
where the world reconstructs itself in silence, in mouths
from which no word is spoken, in the laborious drill of
metal scraping porcelain, and, from somewhere high above,
within the boundaries of the universe, the impression of
once more being called to witness the impossible abundance
of the moment in which life surrenders to devotion, to
the simple, round wholeness, to the agreement inserted
between day and night, between heaven and Earth, when
the world existed hardly at all, or maybe even not at all,
when there was only heaven to make us believe in miracles,
in mystery, in wonder, where there was only heaven to
propel us so far away from one another, to lead us to the fall,
to our descent to Earth, and for us to discover faith and the
other virtues necessary to take us there,

those who return from great sorrow,
those who lose their train of thought,
those who dye their hair,
those who leave on long trips,
those who walk with resignation, bearing sparks of
hope and ignoring the looks that follow or surround them,
moving blindly forward, making up their itinerary on the
spot, wondering where this slow journey will take them,
making themselves feel light and bending to the whims
of the path that lifts them up, lacing the clouds to their
shoes, marking each of their motions with a smile, asking
indulgently for people to let them get by because the road
is so long and their step is so heavy, the ripe hope that fills
them with well-being and confidence, a life that takes your
whole being into custody, the look that is echoed, subdued,
and obedient like a distant abandonment, the space now
faded and trembling in the heat you left behind when you
headed towards your serene, silent, and precise destiny, a
lighthouse sweeping the landscape with its luminous arms,
sweeping up the sound of the waves, the silent, underwater
murmurs of people who speak and cry out in the desert,
those who sing until they are out of breath,
those who utter huge stupidities,
those who carefully lift the blankets off their newborn
to share with you the amazement that overcomes them
every time they look at the masterpiece for which they feel
responsible,
those who do as they please,
those who withdraw into quiet places to share their
secrets, telling the same old stories, trying, once again, to
find a way to change the course of time, looking, during
the pauses, at the drone in the distance, the noise they
have temporarily avoided, unable, as usual, to channel the

flow that is carrying them off, the river being dug, without
their knowledge, in the midst of the crowd staring at them
from afar and from whom they are expecting a sign, a
tender look in which they could lose themselves, in which
they could drown, taking with them to the bottom of the
sea serenity, a moment when life appears as acceptable
evidence, a glorious pact, a mystery through which they
long to cross, where they go adrift despite the reassuring
laughter, complicitous laughter, laughter that reaches them
and pushes them into the flood, the shipwreck they alone
survive, taking with them the heaven they will remember
and pass on to generations to come, the silence where
nothing is said and where endless farewells, before slipping
into the crowd that clamours for you impatiently, call you
to drift away again, to make other plans, and who have no
idea, for the moment, that for one indivisible fraction of
the suspended universe, someone remembered childhood,
the gates of paradise, like a call, a probe, a wild blaze that
sweeps up everything that awaits us after the small talk,
the absentminded introductions, and the noisy opinions
of those who make it their mission to disagree, hoping to
escape as quickly and as far as possible from the essential,
from what keeps us warm, from what holds us together,
from what makes us human in our shared silences, when
we breathe the air we have in common once again and
find once more some common ground, a common cause,
a common desire, a common mode of survival, a common
future somewhere and everywhere it is possible, where
there is still time, where it is still necessary to take a deep
breath as though it were a gift that returns to us, the places
of rest on the shores of the ocean, on the banks of the river,
on the sides of the stream, the places of rest in the middle
of a crowd, of a hum, of a series of movements, the places

of rest in a city, in noisy spots where night puts on its
makeup, in sublime places where heaven's image is reflected
in the Earth's mirror, bringing us back and returning our
life to the starting line, against the face of death like an
explosion, a journey, a destination where we can't help
but refuse unlikely conclusions, if only for a heaven that
holds us in its reins and the way we strive towards its
immense promise, we who have walked far enough and
whose journey has exhausted every refuge save this peace,
the rest we dreamed of in the past, dreamed of until we
wore it out, and which occasionally still rises to the surface
of our memory, in moments as unpredictable as those
of unexpected deliverance, with as many unpredicted,
exhausting, and conclusive contradictions,

those who ask politely about accusations levelled at
them,

those who make public declarations of their love for
their children,

those who call to tell you they're back from a long trip,

those who build trust on the ashes of accumulated
betrayals,

those who apologize for the suffering spread in the
name of unfair and fanatical ideas,

those who offer liquor to those who are doing
everything possible to entertain them,

those who, tactfully and subtly, see to the well-being of
each and every person,

those who take off their shirts to cope with the stifling
heat,

those who meet visitors outside so they won't offend
those close to them,

those who fell from the sky and who are making the
long way back from Earth,

those who ask questions that may never be answered,

those who open their arms to those they promised to never stop loving,

those who ask for the words to the song from those who only know the tune,

those who look outside, trying to escape from the places that seem to imprison them,

those who look after children and wait patiently for their families to come home,

those who cross their fingers, counting the days for their positions to be confirmed,

those who perform complicated tasks without understanding their purpose or outcome,

those who sit, unperturbed, watching the expected collapse of the world they have created for themselves,

those who draw anonymous pleasure from meeting the creator of great works of art,

those who make themselves humble and poor to once more set out on a road where heaven would be their final destination,

those who pick themselves up only to fall back into
the same trap, who imagine that they are brave and pure
only to be faced with the same odour and the same vulgar
words, who pick at the same wounds after nights spent
tripping over themselves, supposing alcohol might be the
secret solution, as an anonymous and discreet wind shakes
the landscape in every direction, who set out along the same
path and pick up their pain to carry it over the clouds, over
the rain, over the strange fascination that is reborn each
time from its own ashes, which gloats, which tells story after
story, which hesitates on the edge of dizziness, broken like
the flow of water which can only swell and widen with time,
who pick themselves up and fall back again, having seen it
happen so often, before coming back with the same excuses,
muttering the same promises and speaking of salvation,
no one can save himself, the old curse that may only apply
to us, we who flee damnation on Earth as in heaven,
which awaits our final rendering, a sometimes improbable
address, a useless compilation of our blessings, the rotation
of interchangeable bodies coming to an end, putting on
our coats and going outside where the air will be clean
and fresh, another autumn soon to announce the coming
of another winter, where we will be delivered in the shiver
that tousles our hair, repeating quietly that we are finally
there and that tonight we shall sleep, delivered and free,
that we will learn to do without certain things, that in truth
we will be able to do without everything from now on, that
life will be returned to its whole and everlasting beatitude,
a bouquet falling from nowhere and landing in the middle
of the road, in the middle of the night, when people will,
certainly, leave us alone to turn off the lights, but we will
know we have arrived and the certainty will fill us with an
effervescent and unexpected joy compared to this night,

a night so simple, this doubtful prayer, not knowing quite what to say, not knowing quite what to do, too busy feeling this lightness, this sought-after version of things that made everything vibrant and overwhelming in its wonder, a secret no one would ever be able to take away from us because how could you tell those who are restless that, on a summer night, somewhere in the universe, in a parking lot on the water's edge, you had a clear and vivid impression of rising up, once and for all, you swore it was true, all the way up there, that heaven had the carefree and casual grace people envy when the wind blows and when you believe that there is still time, that it is still possible to fly away from here, to find ourselves somewhere else,

The Author

Herménégilde Chiasson is one of the best-known poets of the Acadian renaissance and one of Canada's most accomplished cultural icons. He is the author of some thirty plays and almost twenty books, including *Vous* and *Climats*, both shortlisted for the Governor General's Award, and *Conversations*, which won the Governor General's Award for poetry in 1999. He has directed seventeen films, including *Toutes les photos finissent par se ressembler*, *Le Grand Jack*, *Robichaud*, *Épopée*, *Photographies*, and *Ceux qui attendant*, and he has participated in more than a hundred group and solo exhibitions as an artist and curator.

In addition to receiving the Governor General's Award for poetry, Chiasson has been recognized with numerous other honours, including the Prix France-Acadie in 1986 and 1992, two New Brunswick Excellence Awards, the Prix des Terrasses St-Suplice, and the Gascon-Thomas Award from the National Theatre School in 2006. He was made a Chevalier de l'Ordre français des Arts et Lettres and also received the Ordre des francophones d'Amérique, the Grand Prix de la francophonie canadienne, and the Prix quinquennal Antonine-Maillet-Acadie Vie.

Herménégilde Chiasson was born and educated in St-Simon, New Brunswick. He holds degrees from the Université de Moncton, Mount Allison University, State University of New York, and the University of Paris (Sorbonne). He was appointed Lieutenant-Governor of New Brunswick in 2003.

The Translator

Jo-Anne Elder has translated a dozen novels and poetry collections. Among them are many translations of Acadian literature, including three with Fred Cogswell published by Goose Lane Editions: *Unfinished Dreams: Contemporary Poetry of Acadie*, and Herménégilde Chiasson's *Climates* and *Conversations*. Her work was shortlisted for a Governor General's award for translation in 2003. She is also the director of *ellipse*.